PATH 2 STRENGTH

Leader's Guide

Path2Hope Ministries
www.path2hope.org

PATH 2 STRENGTH

PATH2STRENGTH is for Christians everywhere.

This 14-week course is designed to help all Christians quickly accelerate their walk with God, especially those who are feeling weak-hearted, inactive, struggling, or lukewarm, to the point they are passionate, confident, and feeling strong in Him.

The Bible-based lessons incorporated in this booklet are tested and have proven very powerful in the lives of many believers.

This Leader's Guide is designed for small groups.

Over the course of 14 weeks, all participants who are "born again" (no matter how young or old they are in the faith) and complete the lessons should experience real spiritual growth and a clear increase in Spiritual Strength.

We have based this course on the **Names of the Tribes of Israel** and the meanings of their names. The meaning of each Tribe name corresponds to a specific teaching. Each of these teachings is a step on the Path to Strength.

We believe that a Christian who walks through all 14 of these teachings and does all of the action steps will experience a radical shift in their spiritual life and a much closer relationship with God.

GUIDANCE FOR LEADERS

Leaders, welcome to Path2Strength!

You'll be happy to know you don't have to be a master of the spiritual disciplines in order to lead a Path 2 Strength small group.

In fact, this course is designed to allow the leader to grow and be transformed along with the group as you go!

Here is what to know as you lead:

Don't Be Afraid of the Boldness.

Path 2 Strength is designed to be a powerful, transformative study of God's Word and Will for us. In order for those goals to be accomplished, transformational questions have to be asked and answered, energetic conversations must be engaged, and God Himself must be encountered.

And the reward is worth it: Spiritual maturity and strength.

Let the Group Discuss.

Some leaders are tempted to do a lot of the talking, but don't give in! Give group members ample time to answer discussion questions and converse together. If you, the leader, ever find yourself dominating the conversation, try to step back and let the group talk more.

This does not mean you won't participate in the conversations . . . of course you will! It just means a big part of your role is to help balance the conversation and make sure everyone who wants to speak has the opportunity to do so.

It also doesn't mean you don't try to keep the study moving in a timely manner. In order to get through each lesson in a reasonable time frame, we can't spend too much time on any one question. After each question, we have provided tips in parentheses about how many answers generally to entertain. This gives an idea of the flow and time allotted for each.

In summary, create a relaxed atmosphere where whoever wants to participate in the discussion feels free, but where no single person dominates and talks for an extended period of time.

Be Sure to Read Through the Lesson Before the Group Meeting.

It is good practice to read through each lesson at least once or twice before the group meeting and make sure you understand the main points of the teaching and what that particular "step" is about.

Key points are highlighted in the introductory part of the lesson. Pay special attention to these as these are the main takeaways you want to make sure your group understands.

It's Okay to Challenge Your Group in an Encouraging Way, but Don't Pressure Them.

Here's an easy analogy to help understand the right balance:

In farming, we DO want to bust up the soil around a plant to allow its roots to begin growing deep, but we don't want to tug or pull on the plant itself in an attempt to force it to grow.

This means it is great to question general cultural practices and norms that exist in our country and may not be consistent with the life Jesus is calling us to, even and especially within the church. (This is busting up the soil.)

However, it is not good practice to point directly at specific believers in a critical way. (This would be pulling or harming the plant itself.) This includes criticism that may be lobbed at local church leaders who are not present.

Avoid Legalism.

In the Path 2 Strength study, we will be encouraging believers to grow in their obedience and knowledge of God's Law, yet we don't want to do this in a legalistic way. Legalism is when we press other believers to obey the **Letter** of God's Law at the expense of the **Spirit** of God's Law. To obey the Spirit of God's Law is to seek to understand His Heart behind a specific instruction or command so we can grow closer to Him and please Him.

Legalism is the opposite approach. It is the attempt to control others through the application of God's Law to their lives rather than our own.

To keep it simple, let your group members discover the principles in this course and encourage them to allow themselves to be transformed, but don't pressure any group member to make specific changes in their personal practices (unless it pertains to obvious sin).

Let the Holy Spirit transform them in His timing. Give the seeds time to grow.

If they ask you a question about a specific personal practice they have and what you think they should do, some healthy responses can be:

- "Do you feel God leading you to make a change?"

- "Based on what we are learning here, how do you think it applies to your situation?"

- "I am not going to tell you what you should do. That is between you and God. I can only say what I would do if I were in your shoes. So, I'm not going to speak authoritatively, but can share that what I personally would do is _____, and this is why: _____. But again, you have to pray and ask God what He's telling you."

Of course, if they are asking about obvious sins like adultery, theft, lying, drug abuse, etc., you may be clear and gently but firmly explain God's truth about those matters and say you'd like to talk with them more after the session about it.

Provide Feedback to Path2Hope!

Path2Hope Ministries wants to hear feedback as to how your group is doing. We would love to know your recommendations for improving this study as we are always looking for ways to improve its effectiveness!

    We thank you for your heart to lead this group.

    Let the journey begin!

STEP 1

REUBEN - ראובן

"Behold, a Son"

THE WEAKNESS WE ARE STRENGTHENING

Believers are distracted & unfulfilled because Family, Work, & Leisure often have a higher priority than the Kingdom of God.

FOCUS

Correcting Priorities

KEY VERSE

Seek first His kingdom and His righteousness, and all these things will be given to you as well. (Matthew 6:33)

KEY POINTS

- God must be our FIRST priority.
- Jesus did not come to give us a perfect life, financial wealth or a great reputation.
- Jesus came to INVITE us to join Him, to follow Him in His work of expanding His kingdom.
- In response to obedience, God blesses us, in our families, our finances, and in the eyes of others.

The Reuben step is about getting our priorities in the right order. Without this first step, it is very difficult to move into spiritual strength.

The Study

Ice Breaker (20 min)

PLAY "Two Truths & A Lie." Ask each group member to share, in turn:

- A.) Their name
- B.) Why they joined the group, and
- C.) 3 things about themselves. 2 of those things should be true; 1 should be false.

After each person, the group should take a vote on which of the things they think was the "lie"!

(This game is a great intro game for any small group as it helps members get to know each other not just by name, but by personality and motivations.)

Group Discussion (50 min)

1.) ASK: *"What are some of your dreams & aspirations? What are some things you've always wanted to do but haven't done yet?"*

(Try to spend no more than 5 minutes on this question. It is best answered "popcorn-style," with just a few members offering answers, whoever is wanting to share.)

2.) ASK: *"How often do you think about those dreams & aspirations?"*

3.) *Who do you think is more likely to accomplish their dreams, someone who thinks about them often, or someone who rarely thinks about them?*

4.) ASK: *Do you aspire to be closer to God? How often do you think about your relationship with Him?"* (Popcorn-style answers)

5.) **ASK:** *"When you wake up in the morning, what are your first thoughts about? What do our first thoughts reveal about what is most important us in life?"* (Popcorn-style answers)

6.) **ASK the Group to SILENTLY consider the following:** *"Do you always put God first? What activities/events would you be unwilling to cancel in order to put Jesus first?"*

Teaching

The FIRST Step in the Path 2 Strength is the **STEP OF REUBEN.**

Reuben was the first-born son of Jacob and the first Tribe of Israel. The name **Reuben** means "Behold! A Son!"

This is prophetically pointing us to **Look** at **THE Son!** *The Son of God, Jesus, of Nazareth, King of Kings and Lord of Lords!*

7.) **ASK** *"Who is Jesus to you? What do you love most about Him?"* (Spend more time on this question. Encourage people to boldly praise Him for whatever they love about Him - Popcorn-style answers)

8.) **ASK for SILENT Consideration:** *"Isn't Jesus worth being first in your life?*

9.) **READ.** Have different group members read out loud the following passages:

Matthew 6:24 – *"No one can serve two masters; for either he will hate the one and love the other, or else he will be loyal to the one and despise the other. You cannot serve God and mammon [money]."*

Matthew 6:33 – *"Therefore, do not worry, saying, 'What shall we eat?' or 'What shall we drink?' or 'What shall we wear?' For after all these things the Gentiles seek. For your heavenly Father knows that you need all these things. But seek first the kingdom of God and His righteousness, and all these things shall be added to you."*

Luke 14:26 – *"If anyone comes to Me and does not hate his father and mother, wife and children, brothers and sisters, yes, and his own life also, he cannot be My disciple."*

(NOTE: "To hate" in the passage above means "to love less", not "to detest.")

Revelation 3:15-16 – *"I know your works, that you are neither cold nor hot. I could wish you were cold or hot. So then, because you are lukewarm, and neither cold nor hot, I will vomit you out of My mouth."*

Revelation 3:21 – *"To him who overcomes I will grant to sit with Me on My throne, as I also overcame and sat down with My Father on His throne."*

Teaching

Today, many Christians are living for their own dreams and aspirations rather than the Kingdom of God. We have our plans, our goals, and they are our focus. We think constantly about the house we want to have, the blessings we want for our children, the vacations we would like to take, etc. We're often just wanting God to bless whatever it is we personally want to do.

Essentially, we are treating God as if He were some "fertility god." In the ancient world, farmers would go to pagan temples and perform little fertility rituals in order to secure from their idol material blessings over their fields so they could have a better harvest and get more money.

Isn't this actually what too many Christians do? They do their little rituals, go to church, generally behave well, maybe even tithe, all because they want to secure God's blessing over what they want to do. If we do this, we are insulting God and treating Him like a servant rather than our Lord.

This should put the fear of God in us!

For Jesus said, *"because you are lukewarm, and neither cold nor hot, I will vomit you out of My mouth."* (Revelation 3:16) Yet, He also said,

"To him who overcomes I will grant to sit with Me on My throne." (Revelation 3:21a)

God is our Creator. We are supposed to be focused on His Kingdom before our own.

Jesus is calling us to something much higher. In baptism, we died to ourselves and became His. It is time we lived like that – with the Kingdom first before all else. He is calling us to join Him, to follow, to the work of expanding His Kingdom for His glory.

Jesus did not come to provide a way for us to have the perfect family. Jesus calls us to put Him and His Kingdom before our families, and He then responds by blessing our families with peace and blessed relationships.

Jesus did not come to bless us financially. He came to call us to self-sacrifice and generosity. In response, He opens the floodgates of Heavens and promises we will lack for nothing we need.

Jesus did not come to give us the ability to gain honor or a great reputation for ourselves. He calls us to glorify the Father in humility, and in response He lifts us up and honors us.

Behold, the Son! *Behold the Person of Jesus!*

Nothing is more important than Him! He does not exist to serve us; we exist to serve Him. Let us live that way!

10.) ASK: *"During this session, what things did God bring to mind that you may need to change in your life? Are there any places where you may need to reorient your priorities?" (Popcorn-style answers)*

NOTE: Spend a little more time on this question than previous ones – as long as people are willing to talk. This is meat. This is where people are discussing the beginning of their transformation.

Announcement

LET THE GROUP KNOW about the neighborhood outreach this group will be doing at Week 9 of the Path 2 Strength course.

- Choose a date now and ask everyone to mark their calendars (It should be the first Saturday morning (9 am – 12 pm) after the Week 9 (Issachar) lesson.

- Explain the outreach is fun and engaging, and everyone always has a good time.

- Explain that Path2Hope Ministries will be providing adequate training closer to the outreach date so they will be comfortable and feel equipped.

Homework & Action Steps (5 min)

ASSIGN the homework for the coming week! Ask each member to try to complete the following before the next meeting:

Action Step

DECLARE to another believer, tonight or during the week, that from this day forward, you intend to make Jesus & His Kingdom the most important thing in your life.

WORK to make God the first thing you think about each morning as you wake up. *The more you are in love with Him, the easier this is!*

Homework

MEMORIZE Revelation 3:16.

Prayer (10-15 min)

Take a moment to pray for one another. Ask for any major prayer requests and ask certain members of the group to pray for others.

Repeat the requests slowly so everyone hears and those praying aren't embarrassed in the middle of their prayer by forgetting something.

(NOTE: 3 - 4 prayer requests is an ideal number. More than that can be overwhelming for the group to keep up with.)

STEP 2

Simeon - שמעון

"He who Hears/He who Obeys"

The Weakness We Are Strengthening

Too many believers are excusing lives filled with moral compromise. This is harming our relationship with God as well as weakening our witness, both individually and corporately.

Focus

Leaning into Obedience

Key Verse

"If you love Me, keep My commandments." (John 14:15)

Key Points

- God showed His love for us through the gift of salvation, but we show OUR love towards God through Obedience.
- The Law of God remains the perfect expression of God's Heart and still needs to be obeyed.
- Through the sacrifice of Jesus, we are saved and are no longer under the PENALTY of breaking God's law.
- We become more and more like Jesus through obedience. John 14:15 – If you love me, keep my commandments.

The Simeon step is about unblocking our relationship with God by confessing our sins to God and moving into obedience. Without this second step, one's relationship with God is blocked and/or frozen, and the believer will remain in weakness.

The Study

Ice Breaker (10 min)

PLAY "Simon Says." The Group Leader should nominate *someone else* to lead a brief game of Simon Says.

Everyone may remain seated. This game leader should call out commands to the group, sometimes beginning with the phrase "Simon says . . .", sometimes not. Players are supposed to obey only the commands that begin with "Simon says" and not the others.

Players who don't do the "Simon says" commands are "out," as well as players who accidentally obey commands that don't start that way.

As players are eliminated, the game leader should try to go faster and faster until only one player is left! If the group wants to play more than once, and time permits, go for it!

(This game is just fun! Great for this lesson for obvious reasons!)

Review (10 min)

REMIND about the **Step of Reuben**, i.e. prioritizing the Kingdom of God.

1.) Would anyone be willing to recite Revelation 3:16 for us?

2.) Did anyone have any successes or new thoughts over the past week regarding this 1st Step?

Group Discussion (50 min)

Teaching

The SECOND Step in the Path 2 Strength is the **STEP OF SIMEON.**

Simeon was the second-born son of Jacob and the second Tribe of Israel. The name **Simeon** means "He who Hears." In the Bible, "hearing" is always synonymous with "obeying." Jesus often said, "He who has ears to hear, let him hear..." Whenever He said this, He was calling people to obey what He had just said.

For many years, many Christians have emphasized grace at the expense of obedience. This is a major source of our weakness and lukewarmness as a church and in our personal walk.

We correctly understand that through justification by faith, we are saved through the Blood of Jesus and are no longer under the PENALTY of God's Law (for breaking it). However, we often incorrectly teach that this means God's Law is no longer relevant.

Yet, Jesus said, *"For assuredly, I say to you, till heaven and earth pass away, one jot or one tittle will by no means pass from the law till all is fulfilled."* (Matthew 5:18)

Therefore, God's Law remains as the perfect expression of God's Heart and what He desires in our obedience, especially with regards to morality and ethics.

(LEADER'S NOTE: The Old Testament laws regarding **ritual sacrifices** were indeed fulfilled in the final sacrifice of Jesus on the cross. Therefore, the New Testament teaches sacrifices are no longer needed for atonement of sin. **Dietary** laws were loosened by God in the New Testament Book of Acts for the purpose of facilitating missions to the Gentiles. HOWEVER, His *moral* laws are unchanging.)

The PURPOSE of our salvation through the Blood of Jesus is not just to gain entrance to Heaven, but to put us on the path of Sanctification as we become more and more like Jesus, **through obedience**, in order to Glorify God.

Jesus also said, *"If you love Me, keep My commandments."* (John 14:15)

This is very clear. God showed His love *to us* by dying for us and offering us the free gift of salvation. In return, we show Him love by obeying.

We are not saved through obedience – *that is through grace* – but we cannot show love to God back without obedience.

1.) ASK a group member to READ out loud John 13:3-10.

2.) ASK the Group *"What do you think Jesus meant when He told Peter that if He didn't let Him wash his feet, he would have no part with Him?"*

(LEADER'S NOTE: Let the group discuss and try to figure it out, but the correct answer is the washing of the feet is symbolizing regularly confessing our sins to God. We will see that as we take them through the next teaching section.

Jesus was NOT referring to salvation through His blood. When He told Peter that he had already been washed from head to toe, that was referring to being covered in the Blood of Christ and forgiven totally. Here, He just wants to wash the disciples' feet, which is representing daily confession.

Your group does not have to figure this out on their own. Let them discuss, come up with some ideas and then move into the teaching below.)

Teaching

In the Old Testament, outside the Temple of God, there was a bronze altar where the blood sacrifices were made. These sacrifices symbolically pointed forward to the sacrifice of Jesus on the cross for us.

This bronze altar was *outside* the Temple because a person needs to be covered by the blood in order to enter God's house (Temple). However, there was a second object outside the Temple, *a Bronze*

Laver. This was a huge basin filled with water where the priests would wash their hands and feet before entering the Temple.

This is connected to the Lord's Supper where Jesus washed the disciple's feet. It is a symbol for regularly confessing our daily sins to God to get the relationship clear and strong.

As we walk through the world, our feet get dirty, even if we've been bathed before. In the same way, even though we are saved by the Blood of Jesus, we have daily sins that "dirty" our feet.

Just as the priests could not enter God's House without washing their feet, so should we not try to enter God's presence without confessing our daily sins. This would be like insisting on tracking mud through your Father's house when He is offering to clean our feet for us before we come in. This would be extremely disrespectful, so let's not do it.

The Bible actually says our relationship with God will be blocked if we don't do this.

3.) READ. Have different group members read out loud the following passages:

Psalm 66:18 – *"If I regard iniquity in my heart, the Lord will not hear."*

Isaiah 59:2 – *"But your iniquities have separated you from your God; and your sins have hidden His face from you, so that He will not hear."*

1 John 1:9 – *"If we confess our sins, he is faithful and just and will forgive us our sins and purify us from all unrighteousness."*

4.) ASK for SILENT Consideration: *"Are there any sins in your life that you haven't confessed to Him in prayer? (Not just big ones, but even little ones from the last 24 hours.)"*

(LEADER'S NOTE: Let the group sit in silence for about 30 – 45 seconds while they contemplate this. Then, move to the next section.)

Teaching

UNBLOCKING our relationship with God by confessing our sins is only the **1ST HALF** of the **STEP OF SIMEON.**

THE 2ND HALF is moving forward in our walk with Him by obeying *the last thing He asked you to do.*

We often pray for guidance, asking Him to help us know what we should do that day, or tomorrow, or even next year. We pray for guidance with our families, with our careers, and with our ministry, yet we often struggle to hear His answer.

The reason for this is that He has almost always ALREADY asked us to do something that we haven't yet obeyed Him in.

TESTIMONY FROM THE DIRECTOR OF
PATH2HOPE MINISTRIES

> *I remember one time I was praying in a very serious way, asking God to show me how He wanted Path2Hope to grow in the coming year. What were His plans? What did I need to know? How should I lead it?*
>
> *His simple and clear answer to me was, "What about that friend I pressed you to call a few weeks ago that you haven't called yet?"*
>
> *Humbled, I realized I was foolishly asking for "next steps" when I hadn't yet obeyed His previous step for me.*

God will not reveal the next things for us until we've obeyed those previous things He's asked, no matter how simple. It could be as big as beginning to tithe, to change a lifestyle, or launch a ministry. Or it could be as small as texting someone an encouragement.

5.) ASK *"Is there anything you're willing to share that God has been asking you to do that you haven't obeyed yet? (Popcorn-style answers)*

(LEADER'S NOTE: Spend a little more time on this question than previous ones – as long as people are willing to talk. This is strong meat. This is where people are discussing the beginning of their transformation.)

6.) ASK *"Did anything surprise you about this lesson? What idea or teaching do you want to take with you and meditate on strongly this week? (Popcorn-style answers)*

Homework & Action Steps (5 min)

Action Steps

CONFESS all unconfessed sins to God this week. Establish a regular habit of confessing your daily sins to Him. COMMIT to this as a habit.

DECIDE to obey whatever the last thing was He asked of you and then DO it.

Homework

MEMORIZE James 5:16.

Prayer (10-15 min)

Take a moment to pray for one another. Ask for any major prayer requests and ask certain members of the group to pray for others.

Repeat the requests slowly so all hear and those praying aren't embarrassed in the middle of their prayer by forgetting something.

(NOTE: 3 - 4 prayer requests is an ideal number. More than that can be overwhelming for the group to keep up with.)

STEP 3

LEVI - לוי

"My Joining"

THE WEAKNESS WE ARE STRENGTHENING

Too many believers do not spend time with God regularly every day. They either neglect prayer completely, or simply throw up prayers as they go through their day. Their prayers may be ineffective because they're not praising God or confessing sins, or because of disobedience in their lives.

FOCUS

Strengthening our Prayer Life

KEY VERSE

"Pray without ceasing."
(1 Thessalonians 5:17)

KEY POINTS

- Prayer is a NON-NEGOTIABLE habit for a follower of Christ.
- Prayer takes us the closest to God's presence.
- Prayer is the way we tap into the POWER of God.
- A believer cannot live without prayer. It is the first spiritual habit that a believer needs to develop.
- There are four different elements of prayer: *Praise, Confession of Sins, Prayer for Others* and *Prayer for Self.*

The Step of Levi is about establishing a strong Habit of Prayer in a believer's life. Believers should move away from vain repetitions of words or from merely casting up prayers throughout the day, and **instead begin a habit of a purposeful quiet time alone with the Lord each morning before doing anything else.**

The Study

Review (5 – 10 min)

REMIND about the **STEP OF SIMEON**, i.e. increasing obedience.

1.) Did anyone have any successes or new thoughts over the past week regarding this 2nd Step?

Ice Breaker (15 min)

ASK *"What is the most memorable activity/vacation you did with your family as a child?"*

(Everyone answers, going in a circle.)

Group Discussion (50 min)

1.) ASK *Did that family activity or event make you feel more connected, more "joined" to your family? Why or how did it make you feel more connected? (2 or 3 popcorn answers)*

(Leader's Note: The purpose of this question is to get to the realization that it is by spending time and/or sharing experience with others that we connect with them. Thus, to connect with God we must spend intentional time with Him.)

Teaching

The THIRD Step in the Path 2 Strength is the **STEP OF LEVI.**

The name Levi means "Joiner" or "My Joining." Just as spending quality time with your family joins you closer to them, so does spending quality time with the Father join us closer to Him.

Therefore, the Step of Levi is to establish a strong prayer habit in your life.

2.) ASK *If you had to guess, what do you feel the majority of Christians' prayer lives look like? Do you feel the Church as a whole is doing well with prayer or not? (2 or 3 popcorn answers)*

3.) ASK *How is your personal prayer life right now? If we are honest, what are some of our struggles/obstacles when it comes to prayer? (2 or 3 popcorn answers)*

Teaching

For some, prayer is a habit that comes easy. For others, it is a struggle. A habit they are not drawn to engage in. Sometimes we doubt its power, and so neglect it. Sometimes, God seems silent, and so we feel dead in our walk.

Nevertheless, prayer is a non-negotiable habit for a follower of Jesus. The Gospels show us that Jesus spent a significant amount of time praying, talking with His Father.

4.) READ: Have different group members read out loud the following passages:

Matthew 14:23 – "After He had sent the crowds away, He went up on the mountain by Himself to pray; and when it was evening, He was there alone."

Mark 1:3 – "In the early morning, while it was still dark, Jesus got up, left the house, and went away to a secluded place, and was praying there."

Luke 5:16 – "But Jesus Himself would often slip away to the wilderness and pray."

Teaching

Even though Jesus was already intimately connected to His Father, He felt the need to spend a lot of time with Him alone. You could even say He longed to spend time with His Father more than anyone else.

So, if we are to imitate Him, we *must* pray.

And Jesus taught us there is a right way to pray and a wrong way to pray.

As Jesus said, *"And when you pray, do not use vain repetitions as the heathen do. For they think that they will be heard for their many words."* (Matthew 6:7)

This means we are not to just *repeat* the Lord's Prayer over and over, or any other repeated phrases, but we are to be sharing our true heart with Him, to connect with Him, to JOIN with Him.

God teaches us how to pray in many different ways. From the words of the Lord's Prayer, to symbolism encoded in nature and in the furniture in God's Temple, He's revealed truth about prayer in many different ways.

In ancient Israel, worship of God was conducted first at a large tent structure called the Tabernacle and then later at a very beautiful Temple. Both were built according to a pattern God had shown Moses on Mount Sinai and they symbolized God's House, i.e. where He dwelled among His people. He encoded a lot of symbolism in its details.

Inside God's House (the Temple), there were only three fixtures (pieces of furniture) that lay in the approach to God's presence behind the Veil in a place called the Holy of Holies. These three fixtures represented *the* three ways we seek or approach God.

Among them was the Golden Altar of Incense. Scripture tells us this altar symbolized the prayers of the saints:

> "Then another angel . . . came and stood at the altar. He was given much incense, that he should offer it with the prayers of all the saints upon the golden altar which was before the throne."
> (Revelation 8:3)

This Altar of Incense was located *closest* to God's Throne. **This means that prayer takes us closest to His presence.**

Now let's talk about nature, because God also teaches us things symbolically through nature. **In Creation, God made trees to symbolize believers rooted in the Kingdom of God.**

5.) **ASK** *What three things does a tree need to survive?*

(**Leader's Note:** Let the group try to answer this question for a minute, but the correct answer is **Water, Sunlight, and Soil.**)

Teaching

A tree has to have water, soil, and sunlight to survive. If a tree is deprived of any of these three things for an extended period of time, it suffers.

Now, **Fresh Water** *is always a symbol for God's* **Power** *in Scripture.* **And Prayer is the way we tap into that power.**

A tree's need for water teaches us just how important prayer is for a believer.

As trees cannot live without water, so a believer cannot live without prayer. As a seed is first activated by water, so is prayer the first habit a believer needs to develop. Of course, this habit begins by a person confessing their sins to God in prayer and asking for forgiveness through the Blood of Jesus. This is the activation of the seed.

6.) **ASK** a group member to read Matthew 6:33.

> But Seek FIRST the kingdom of God and His righteousness, and all these things shall be added to you.

7.) **ASK** the group to SILENTLY consider the following for a moment:

We know that prayer is one of the primary ways we seek God. Therefore, in light of Matthew 6:33, can we honestly claim to be seeking God FIRST before all else if a time of prayer is the not the FIRST thing we do each day?

Teaching

Putting God first means showing Him he's first by seeking His face in prayer before getting the kids ready, before eating breakfast, before work, before anything.

If we don't do that, then it means those other things are first.

There's really no way to dance around it or deny it. If an outsider looking in at your life cannot see God is first through your daily habits, how could you claim to them He's first at all?

And early morning prayer is an amazing blessing. It sets your day right. It gets you connected to your Loving Father before the stresses of the day have time to set in.

God has also shown us that there should be different elements in our prayers.

Four *different elements to be precise:*

- *Praise*
- *Confession of Sins*
- *Prayer for Others*
- *Prayer for Self*

The Lord's Prayer contains all four of these elements, and we also see them in the symbolism encoded in the 4 fragrances combined in the incense used in God's Temple. (For more information on this, see Appendix A.)

8.) **ASK** *Why do you think it's important to begin prayer with Praise?*

9.) **ASK** *Why is it important to include Confession of Sins in our daily prayers?*

10.) **ASK** *Why is it important to always include a Prayer for Others before Self?*

Rejoice always, pray continually, give thanks in all circumstances; for this is God's will for you in Christ Jesus.
(1 Thessalonians 5:16-18)

Homework & Action Steps (5 min)

ASSIGN the homework for the coming week! Ask each member to try to complete the following before the next meeting:

Action Steps

COMMIT to a daily PRAYER habit. BEGIN each day for the next seven days in Prayer, using the 4 Elements of prayer. Always pray your heart and share your true feelings and thoughts with Him.

Homework

MEMORIZE the Lord's Prayer. (Matthew 6:9-13)

Prayer (10-15 min)

Take a moment to pray for one another. Ask for any major prayer requests and ask certain members of the group to pray for others.

Repeat the requests slowly so everyone hears and those praying aren't embarrassed in the middle of their prayer by forgetting something.

(NOTE: 3 - 4 prayer requests is an ideal number. More than that can be overwhelming for the group to keep up with.)

STEP 4

JUDAH - יהודה

"Praise, Let Him Be Praised"

THE WEAKNESS WE ARE STRENGTHENING

Many who describe themselves as Christian simultaneously criticize and avoid what they call "organized religion." Others have fallen out of fellowship in a local church, not considering the **Habit of Fellowship** something that needs to be urgently fixed. The result is a weakened Body of Christ and millions of Christians who are not only backsliding but often feel alone and hopeless as well.

FOCUS

Strengthening Fellowship in the Body

KEY VERSE

*"And let us consider how we may spur one another on toward love and good deeds, **not giving up meeting together**, as some are in the habit of doing, but encouraging one another—and all the more as you see the Day approaching."* (Hebrews 10:24-25)

KEY POINTS

- The church (fellow believers) is the BRIDE of Christ.
- Fellowship is 1 of the 3 NON-NEGOTIABLE habits of a believer.
- A Christian who intentionally separates himself from fellowship (organized religion) is like a branch that cuts itself off from the vine. Left with no power, no life flowing through it. No longer part of the plan. ***Useless*** in the growing of the Kingdom of God.
- We are blessed through fellowship, and God is praised in many ways when we come together in unity.

The Step of Judah is about establishing a strong Habit of Fellowship in a believer's life. Believers should understand that to be separated from the Body is to be separated from Him. We should ensure we are in fellowship with other believers at least once per week if not more.

The Study

Review (5 – 10 min)

1.) Would anyone like to take a stab at reciting the Lord's Prayer?

REMIND about the **STEP OF LEVI**, i.e. establishing a Habit of Prayer.

2.) Did anyone have any successes or new thoughts over the past week regarding this 3rd Step?

Ice Breaker (20 min)

PLAY Would you rather . . . ?

(The small group leader can ask each person in the group a different question. Give time for brief comments on each answer, but make sure each person has a chance to answer a question and that a variety of questions are asked.)

- Visit the doctor or the dentist?
- Eat broccoli or carrots?
- Watch TV or listen to music?
- Own a lizard or a snake?
- Have a beach holiday or a mountain holiday?
- Be an apple or a banana?
- Be invisible or be able to read minds?
- Be hairy all over or completely bald?
- Be the most popular or the smartest person you know?
- Make headlines for saving somebody's life or winning a Nobel Prize?
- Go without television or fast food for the rest of your life?
- Have permanent diarrhea or permanent constipation?
- Be handsome/beautiful and dumb or be ugly and really smart?

- Always be cold or always be hot?
- Not hear or not see?
- Eliminate hunger and disease or be able to bring lasting world peace?
- Be stranded on a deserted island alone or with someone you don't like?
- See the future or change the past?
- Be three inches taller or three inches shorter?
- Wrestle a lion or fight a shark?

Group Discussion (50 min)

Teaching

John Piper is a well-known and respected pastor who has written many powerful books. Once, when he was speaking about Christian missions and missionary activity, he said, "*"Missions exist because worship doesn't."*

1.) ASK *What did John Piper mean by that?*

LEADER'S NOTE: Be ready to guide the conversation in the right direction as needed. John Piper's point was that the purpose of Christian missions is to create more worshippers of God through evangelism and discipleship. His quote is elevating the importance of worship in life.

Teaching

Zack Mason, the Executive Director of Path2Hope Ministries, says, "**The purpose of life is to glorify God and worship Him** – and we were designed to worship corporately together in fellowship, not just individually."

Yet, the majority of self-described Christians in the United States today do not attend church regularly, if at all.

2.) ASK *Have you ever heard someone say something similar to, "I love Jesus, I just don't want anything to do with organized religion"? If so, when?* (2 or 3 popcorn answers)

Yet, the Bible says the Church is the Bride of Christ.

Can you imagine a person walking up to a man and saying, "Man, I love you, love to hang out with you, but I hate your wife. Please keep her away from me."? *That friendship probably wouldn't survive the conversation.*

Yet, this is what many self-described "Christians" say to Jesus: "Love you, Jesus, but I don't want anything to do with your Bride!"

3.) ASK *Why do you think so many Christians avoid church?* (2 or 3 popcorn answers)

4.) ASK *Do you think this lack of church attendance has made the American Church stronger or weaker?*

5.) ASK *Have you ever been hurt by someone in the Church before? What was your reaction? Did it impact your church attendance?* (2 or 3 popcorn answers)

6.) ASK *What about a positive influence? Tell some stories about Christians who invested in you or made you feel loved or worthwhile.* (2 or 3 popcorn answers)

Teaching

Zack Mason tells a story about when he was young:

> *Next to my father, my middle school youth pastor probably had more influence on me, spiritually speaking, than anyone else in my life. Unfortunately, as I entered high school, my youth pastor and several members of his young family suddenly found themselves passing through some very difficult health circumstances. In the middle of this crisis, for a reason that is still not known to me, my church decided to terminate his employment.*

Needless to say, the youth group scattered. I personally did not attend church again for at least 5 years. From 9th grade until my second year of college, I did not attend church anywhere and agreed with everyone that "the church was full of hypocrites."

Nevertheless, I continued to seek God on my own and read the Bible, and I prayed every single day. I read all the way through the Bible at least 5 times during that period.

Then, one day, God spoke to me and said, **"Zack, you don't go to church for other people, you go to church for Me!"**

That made it clear to me how important fellowship was to Him, how much He cared about it, and I've been back in church ever since.

7.) **ASK** What do you think God might have meant by 'you go to church for Me'?

8.) **READ:** Have different group members read out loud the following passages:

Acts 2:42- "They devoted themselves to the apostles' teaching **and to fellowship**, to the breaking of bread and to prayer."

1 Thessalonians 5:11 - "Therefore encourage one another and build one another up, just as you are doing."

Hebrews 10:24-25 - "And let us consider how we may spur one another on toward love and good deeds, **not giving up meeting together**, as some are in the habit of doing, but encouraging one another—and all the more as you see the Day approaching."

Teaching

Fellowship is one of the 3 non-negotiable habits of a believer!

Have you ever seen a Jewish *Menorah?* Menorahs are replicas of the original Golden Lampstand in God's Temple in the Old Testament.

God commanded the original Golden Lampstand be placed in His Temple because it symbolized believers unified in one body. It had seven branches. Six of the branches (we'll recall the Book of Revelation says six is the number of man) branched out of the seventh, central branch that rose taller than the other six. This pictures us as believers abiding in Christ. It also shows that apart from Him we can do nothing.

God instructed Moses regarding its construction, saying:

> *"... Their branches shall be of one piece;*
> *all of it shall be one hammered piece of pure gold."*
> (Exodus 25:36)

So, we see God specifically required that the Menorah could not be made of multiple pieces of gold hammered together. It had to be a single, solid piece of gold from the start, formed into its shape by a master craftsman.

This teaches us about the spiritual concept of unity within the Body of Christ. We are one with Christ and one with each other. We must operate as one Body!

Teaching

Scripture teaches us that we are *all* part of the Body of Christ, and that Jesus is our Head. Can you imagine a person saying to Jesus, "I love your head, Jesus, but I want nothing to do with your body!"

In the previous session, we learned that, in nature, God designed trees as an intentional symbol for believers rooted in His Kingdom. We also learned that a tree's need for water points us to our need for regular prayer.

Yet, that is not all trees need! They also need soil!

Trees rooted in the soil represent Christians rooted in fellowship with the Kingdom of God.

9.) ASK *How well will a tree do if it refuses to be rooted in soil?*

You can water a tree all you want, but if its roots are pointed up in the air, it's going to wither.

A "Christian" who intentionally separates themselves from "organized religion" is like a branch that cuts itself off from the vine.

No power. No life flowing through it. No future. No longer part of the plan. Of no use whatsoever, except for the fire. (John 15:6)

So, fellowship is essential!

NOTE: The soil must be healthy soil! Poisonous soil will also hurt or kill a tree.

Yet, we are also not looking for *perfect* soil. As Kevin Myers of 12Stone Church says, *"If you find the perfect church, don't attend because you'll mess it up."*

10.) READ: Ask a group member to read out loud the following PRAYER OF JESUS in the Gospel of John:

John 17:20-23 – "My prayer is not for them alone. I pray also for those who will believe in me through their message, that all of them may be one, Father, just as you are in me and I am in you. May they also be in us so that the world may believe that you have sent me. I have given them the glory that you gave me, that they may be one as we are one— I in them and you in me—so that they may be brought to complete unity. Then the world will know that you sent me and have loved them even as you have loved me."

11.) ASK *What are many of the reasons or benefits you can think of why fellowship is important? Why does God care about it so much? Why should we care about it?* (5 or 6 popcorn answers)

LEADER'S NOTE: This is an important question. It's okay to take a little more time on it.

Teaching

The FOURTH Step in the Path 2 Strength is the **STEP OF JUDAH.**

The name of Judah means "Praised" or "Let Him be praised!"

When we come together in fellowship, we lift up powerful praise to Him together in worship!

We receive blessings through fellowship because opportunities (jobs, housing, etc.) come through people, i.e. other Christians. In other words, fellowship helps us get our needs met. These blessings then cause us to praise Him too.

We are also blessed through fellowship because God corrects us and speaks wisdom to us through other Christians. This produces a more blessed life in us, and so we praise Him!

In fellowship, we learn wisdom and come to know we are not alone, that others care for us. Through them, we feel God's love for us in tangible ways, and so we praise Him!

In fellowship, we learn how to coordinate with other believers as a team, each one of us using their spiritual gifts and fulfilling their God-given purpose, and so we praise Him!

And so, God is praised in many ways when we come together in unity, in fellowship.

The Step of Judah is about establishing a strong Habit of Fellowship in a believer's life. Believers should understand that to be separated from the Body is to be separated from Him. We should ensure we are in fellowship with other believers at least once per week if not more.

Homework & Action Steps (5 min)

ASSIGN the homework for the coming week! Ask each member to try to complete the following before the next meeting:

Action Steps

COMMIT to regular, weekly fellowship. If you're not already attending a church weekly for worship, begin doing so.

COMMIT also to staying in a small group of some kind after completing this Path2Strength semester.

Homework

MEMORIZE Hebrews 10:24-25:

"And let us consider how we may spur one another on toward love and good deeds, **not giving up meeting together***, as some are in the habit of doing, but encouraging one another—and all the more as you see the Day approaching."* (Hebrews 10:24-25)

Prayer (10-15 min)

Take a moment to pray for one another. Ask for any major prayer requests and ask certain members of the group to pray for others.

Repeat the requests slowly so everyone hears and those praying aren't embarrassed in the middle of their prayer by forgetting something.

(NOTE: 3 - 4 prayer requests is an ideal number. More than that can be overwhelming for the group to keep up with.)

STEP 5

DAN - דן

"Judge"

THE WEAKNESS WE ARE STRENGTHENING

Many Christians do not read the Bible regularly. This has caused great **weakness** in the Body of Christ.

FOCUS

Establishing a regular Bible-reading Habit.

KEY VERSE

"All Scripture is God-breathed and is useful for teaching, rebuking, correcting and training in righteousness."
(2 Timothy 3:16)

KEY POINTS

- A regular Bible Habit is the 3rd NON-NEGOTIABLE habit of a believer.
- God's Word governs our lives.
- God's Word is FOOD for our soul. We must be constantly feeding our soul, or we will become spiritually weak.
- 2 Timothy 3:16: *All Scripture is God-breathed and is useful for teaching, rebuking, correcting and training in righteousness.*

The Step of Dan is about establishing a strong Habit of Bible-reading in a believer's life. God speaks back to us primarily through His Word.

Leader's Note

Please do a little EXTRA preparation by making yourself familiar with the material that follows which is not in the participant's guide!

As group leader, it is good to ask yourself and understand **why** more Christians don't read the Bible regularly:

Common Obstacles

1.) They think they can't/won't understand it.

This can be because they grew up in a church that discouraged Bible reading, or it can be because they've tried to read it before and did not understand very well.

A good approach is to emphasize that **God's Word is like our spiritual food.** We need it daily just as we need food daily, *and just as we don't have to tell our stomachs how to digest a sandwich, so we don't have to tell our soul how to digest Scripture that it takes in.*

The important thing is to be reading daily and don't worry about understanding it or not. Eventually the Christian will understand more and more. In the meantime, their soul knows what to do with it.

Also, keep in mind that a ***non-believer*** will **not** get the same spiritual value out of the Word. *Only believers can truly understand it.*

2.) They're not convinced it's important.

This is the focus of this lesson, to help the believer see how essential it is.

3.) They can't seem to find time. Life is too busy.

This is about priorities. A Christian who has God as the first and most important thing in their heart WILL make time to read His Word every day. A person not having time reveals in a very simple way that God has a secondary role in their life.

4.) They secretly think it will be boring.

Of course, this is not true. The Bible is very intellectually stimulating, but they need to begin reading to find that out. Ultimately, this is a heart issue as they are not willing to endure "boredom" for Him.

5.) They secretly don't want to have to change their lifestyle, i.e. they suspect the Bible might require them to live differently.

Yep. They're right about that one.

Helping A Believer Diagnose Their Weakness

If a Christian is feeling *weak*, it means they need to be reading the Bible.

Prayer is not enough. ***Prayer is like spiritual breathing.*** We *must* breathe constantly, but if all we do in life is breathe – ***if we never eat*** – *we will grow weak.*

The Bible is like our spiritual food, so we must partake of it regularly to remain strong.

Therefore, if a believer is feeling overwhelmed, like they are suffocating, it means they need to pray, but if they feel weak, they need to read the Word.

The Study

Review (5 – 10 min)

1.) ASK Would anyone like to take a stab at reciting Hebrews 10:24-25?

REMIND about the **STEP OF JUDAH**, i.e. establishing a Habit of Fellowship.

2.) Did anyone have any successes or new thoughts over the past week regarding this 4th Step?

Ice Breaker (20 min)

PLAY: <u>Word Pictures</u>

GIVE 3 - 4 people in the group a piece of paper. They should each write a funny or unusual sentence at the top of their paper.

Then, each person hands their piece of paper to the person on their left. Now everyone will have a new piece of paper.

The individuals now holding the papers should draw pictures that represent the already written sentence to them. Next, they should fold the paper over so the original sentence is hidden and only the new picture can be seen.

They pass the papers to the left again. This third person will write out a sentence that describes the picture to them and then fold the paper over so the second person's picture is what is hidden now and only the sentence written by the third person can be seen.

Again, pass to the left. The game alternates between people drawing and writing out sentences of what they see as they continue passing each paper to the left.

The icebreaker ends when each person receives their original paper. Let everyone share their original sentence and the final sentence or picture.

This game is a variation on the old party game "Operator" or "Rumor Mill."

Group Discussion (50 min)

3.) **ASK** *During the game we just played, what would be the only way to ensure the final sentence matched the original sentence?*

(This is a question for brief consideration more than anything, but the leader can allow 2-3 quick popcorn answers.)

Teaching

The only real way to make *sure* the final sentence matches the original sentence is to show the other players the original sentence and ask them to copy it!

Once we lose access to an original message, it invariably gets garbled over time as people add their own flavor to it, forget some of the original words and try to fill them in themselves, or even make something up that sounds better to their ears.

This is what happens in cultures too. **Once people lose access to the original Word of God, we as individuals, and as a society together, begin to drift pretty quickly.**

We have seen this patter repeat many times over the ages.

4.) **READ:** Ask group members to read the following verses:

Judges 17:6: – *"In those days Israel had no king; everyone did as they saw fit."*

Judges 21:25 – *"In those days Israel had no king; everyone did as they saw fit."*

Deuteronomy 12:8 – *"You are not to do as we do here today, everyone doing as they see fit."*

Proverbs 14:12 – *"There is a way that seems right to a man, But its end is the way of death."*

In Ancient Israel, there were times when they not only didn't have a king, but they were not governing themselves with the Word of God. As Proverbs 14:12 says, this leads to death.

> **5.) ASK** *Can you share a time that you or someone you know did not follow the principles of the Bible and it cost them?* (2 or 3 popcorn answers)

Teaching

Many people want to hear from God.

Many people often also voice a frustration with not "hearing Him" when they pray. They complain that they've prayed and prayed and haven't gotten answers to questions or their requests fulfilled.

This inevitably leads to some believers becoming frustrated with their prayer lives. Yet, what if we are not understanding certain principles of how God communicates?

> **6.) ASK** *In your experience, has God spoken to you more clearly during prayer or through Bible reading?* (2 or 3 popcorn answers)

Teaching

While God does speak to us sometimes directly through prayer, most often prayer is about us sharing our heart with Him. Speaking to Him. When He does speak back to us, it is almost always in the form of a gentle whisper which takes years of spiritual practice and discipline to discern.

He also speaks to us through other believers in fellowship, **but He primarily speaks to us through the Bible.** *The Bible is the way He most often speaks back to us.*

People often complain that they want to hear from God, they want to hear what He has to say, but they don't want to spend time reading what He has already spoken!

7.) ASK *Think about this for a minute silently. Why would God spend time speaking to someone through prayer who doesn't care to read what He's already said?*

Teaching

Regular Bible study is the 3rd non-negotiable habit every believer must do to seek God well.

In God's Temple, the Golden Table of Showbread symbolized the Word of God. *Bread is always a symbol for "teaching" or "God's Word" in Scripture.*

Because the Table of Showbread is one of the three fixtures that lie in the approach to God's presence, it is confirmed that God's Word is one of the three essential habits.

The Bible says there were twelve loaves of bread presented on the table, all prepared without yeast. Twelve is the number of Godly government, so this shows that ***God's Word shall govern our lives.*** In Scripture, yeast is a symbol for sinful pride which "puffs up", **so we should always approach God's Word with humility and without adding to it.**

In Creation, trees, which are God's symbols for believers, need sunlight to survive and grow just as much as they need water and soil. **Light is always a symbol for truth.** And the sun is a symbol for Christ, the Son of God. So, **sunlight represents the truth of Christ,** or the truth of God's Word.

Just as a person cannot walk through a pitch-black room without stumbling over furniture, so can we not walk through life without the light of truth. We need truth to navigate life without getting hurt.

Therefore, Bible-reading is essential!

8.) **ASK** *What are some of the reasons you think Christians don't read the Bible more? What are our answers to those obstacles?* (5 or 6 popcorn answers)

LEADER'S NOTE: The group leader should be prepared to give a good response to these common reasons for not reading the Bible. Please review the "Obstacles" section in the Leader's Notes for this lesson.

As group leader, you should also bring up any of the common reasons listed in the "Obstacles" section that the group doesn't think of on their own.

LEADER'S NOTE: The "Obstacles" section addresses common reasons *believers* don't read the Bible more. Non-believers don't read the Bible because they don't trust its accuracy or that it's God's Word. For answers to these objections, please refer individuals to any of the following resources:

1.) **Is the Bible Reliable?**
https://www.christianity.com/wiki/bible/is-the-bible-reliable-the-evidence-we-know-so-far.html

2.) **The Exodus Case** *by Lennart Moller*

3.) **The Case for Christ** *by Lee Stroebel*

4.) **Testimony of the Evangelists** *by Simon Greenleaf*

5.) **The Signature of God** *by Grant R. Jeffrey*

6.) **Evidence that Demands a Verdict** *by Josh McDowell*

7.) **How Do You Know You're Not Wrong** *by Paul Copan*

(There are many other similar books. If you need more resources, please contact Path2Hope for additional references.)

Teaching

The FIFTH Step in the Path 2 Strength is the **STEP OF DAN.**

The name of Dan means "Judge," referring to a judge over disputes, or it can also simply mean "a leader", i.e. a governing leader.

Therefore, the Step of Dan is about placing God's Word as the judge and leader over our lives.

Diagnosing Ourselves

Prayer is like spiritual breathing. If we don't breathe, we pretty quickly begin to *suffocate*. A feeling that is very overwhelming.

So, if a believer is feeling overwhelmed – like they are spiritually *suffocating* – it means they need to pray. Yet feeling spiritually **overwhelmed** is not the same thing as feeling spiritually **weak.**

That's because prayer by itself is not enough. While we *must* breathe constantly, if all we ever do in life is breathe – ***if we never eat*** – we will grow *weak.*

The Bible is like our spiritual food, so we must partake of it regularly to remain strong. Therefore, whenever a Christian is feeling spiritually weak, it means they need to be reading MORE of the Bible than they currently are.

In summary, if a believer is feeling overwhelmed, like they are suffocating, it means they need to pray, but if they feel weak, they need to read more of the Word.

The Step of Dan is about establishing a strong Habit of Bible-reading in a believer's life. God speaks back to us primarily through His Word.

Homework & Action Steps (5 min)

ASSIGN the homework for the coming week! Ask each member to try to complete the following before the next meeting:

Action Steps

COMMIT to regular daily Bible reading FIRST thing every morning in conjunction with prayer time.

If you don't know *where* to start, we have included a Bible-Reading Plan for you at the end of this book.

MEMORIZE 2 Timothy 3:16

Prayer (10-15 min)

Take a moment to pray for one another. Ask for any major prayer requests and ask certain members of the group to pray for others.

Repeat the requests slowly so everyone hears and those praying aren't embarrassed in the middle of their prayer by forgetting something.

(NOTE: 3 - 4 prayer requests is an ideal number. More than that can be overwhelming for the group to keep up with.)

STEP 6

NAPHTALI - נפתלי

"My Struggling"

THE WEAKNESS WE ARE STRENGTHENING

Many Christians are hanging out in the church's "hospital." They know Jesus came for the sick, not the healthy, but they don't understand Jesus calls us to get well and move into health, not remain in the ER. Most Christians are not pursuing holiness.

FOCUS

Beginning to pursue obedience daily.

KEY VERSE

Therefore, if anyone cleanses himself from the latter, he will be a vessel for honor, sanctified and useful for the Master, prepared for every good work.
(2 Timothy 2:21)

KEY POINTS

- Sanctification, the 2nd part of Salvation is the process of becoming HOLY and saved from the "World."
- Holiness does not mean purity, it means "SET APART." The opposite of holy is not "impure," but "common."
- To be "Set Apart" means to live our lives each day trying to become more and more like Jesus, to be separate from the World so God can use us for His special purposes.
- Living "Set Apart" is a struggle, but we can overcome because Christ is with us to help and guide us.

The Step of Naphtali is about intentionally entering the Path of Holiness, recognizing our special purpose in Him, and establishing a strong Habit of Long Obedience.

The Study

Review (5 – 10 min)

REMIND about the **Step of Dan**, i.e., establishing a Habit of Bible Study first thing in the morning.

1.) **ASK** So, how many days this last week were you able to add Bible reading to your morning quiet time? If not all 7, what got in the way?

Ice Breaker (20 min)

ASK *What are some physical characteristics, personality traits, or habits you received from your parents you wish you could change? Are there any you love and want to always keep?*

(Everyone answers, in a circle)

Group Discussion (50 min)

Teaching

The SIXTH Step in the Path 2 Strength is the **Step of Naphtali.**

The name Naphtali, the 6th born son of Israel, means "My Struggle." Once a Christian has become a follower of the Messiah, their lifelong struggle is to become more and more like Him over the course of the days God has given them.

Many Christians are not aware the Bible teaches there are *three* parts of salvation: ***Justification, Sanctification, and Glorification.***

Justification is the first (1st) part of Salvation, and it means to be made just, to be declared "innocent" in God's court. This is a **legal**

declaration, a one-time thing, and because it's a *legal declaration*, it cannot be undone or taken back.

Here are some verses about Justification you can look up later: Romans 3:28, Romans 5:1, Romans 5:9, 1 Cor. 6:11, Titus 3:7

We are justified in God's eyes in this way when we accept the free pardon He has offered us through the Blood of Christ. When we accept Jesus as our Lord & Savior, we put on His righteousness and God no longer sees our transgressions, only the holiness of Christ.

To be Justified means to be saved from Hell.

Glorification, the last (3rd) part of Salvation, is the moment when we receive our glorified bodies in Heaven after death. This is different from being saved from hell, this is to be saved from our fallen Flesh, i.e. all human desires.

Here are some verses about Glorification you can look up later: Romans 8:30, Philippians 3:20-21

The middle (2nd) part of Salvation is Sanctification. Sanctification is a process that takes our entire life to complete. It is to be saved from the World as we become more and more like Jesus.

2.) **ASK** *How does understanding the three parts of Salvation (Justification, Sanctification, Glorification) help you navigate the Christian life? Does it help you explain the Christian walk to others more easily?* (2-3 popcorn answers)

Teaching

Sanctification, the 2nd part of Salvation, is the focus of the **STEP OF NAPHTALI.**

But what exactly does the word "Sanctification" mean?

To be sanctified is to be made holy. The Bible calls you and me *saints*. However, the word *saint* doesn't mean super righteous person, or an extremely pure person. Holiness does not mean purity; it means *to be set apart*.

Therefore, the opposite of Holy is not impure, it is common.

To be holy to God means to be set apart for a special purpose for Him. Of course, this would hopefully include keeping oneself clean of unclean things, *but to be holy means to be special.*

An easy way to understand this is to think about how many families have special plates and silverware in their china cabinets they only take out for Christmas and Easter. These are *special* plates that will not be used for *common* things.

3.) ASK *Can you think of any other examples of things we consider common vs. special in the world?* (2-3 popcorn answers)

Teaching

Now, would a normal person take a fine china plate out of their cabinet and use it as a doggie bowl?

(Pause and think silently about this for a moment.)

Of course, the answer is no.

Then, what about us? God has called us holy and asks us to pursue holiness.

To be holy means to act in a way that is consistent with the special purpose God has already called you to.

4.) ASK *If you had to explain to another Christian why we should pursue holiness, what would you tell them?* (2-3 popcorn answers)

5.) **READ:** Ask group members to read the following verses:

2 Timothy 2:15-16;19-21 – *"Be diligent to present yourself approved to God, a worker who does not need to be ashamed, rightly dividing the word of truth. But shun profane and idle babblings, for they will increase to more ungodliness . . . Nevertheless, the solid foundation of God stands, having this seal: "The Lord knows those who are His," and, "Let everyone who names the name of Christ depart from iniquity." But in a great house there are not only vessels of gold and silver, but also of wood and clay, some for honor and some for dishonor. Therefore, if anyone cleanses himself from the latter, he will be a vessel for honor,* **sanctified** *and useful for the Master, prepared for every good work."*

2 Timothy 2:22-26 – *"Flee also youthful lusts; but pursue righteousness, faith, love, peace with those who call on the Lord out of a pure heart. But avoid foolish and ignorant disputes, knowing that they generate strife. And a servant of the Lord must not quarrel but be gentle to all, able to teach, patient, in humility correcting those who are in opposition, if God perhaps will grant them repentance, so that they may know the truth, and that they may come to their senses and escape the snare of the devil, having been taken captive by him to do his will."*

Leviticus 11:44a – *"For I am the Lord your God. You shall therefore consecrate yourselves, and you shall be holy; for I am holy."*

1 Thessalonians 4:7 – *"For God did not call us to uncleanness, but in holiness."*

1 Peter 1:14-16 – *"[Be] as obedient children, not conforming yourselves to the former lusts, as in your ignorance; but as He who called you is holy, you also be holy in all your conduct, because it is written, "Be holy, for I am holy."*

Luke 6:47-48 – *"As for everyone who comes to me and hears my words* **and puts them into practice***, I will show you what they are like. They are like a man building a house, who dug down deep and laid the* *foundation on rock. When a flood came, the torrent struck that house but could not shake it, because it was well built."*

John 14:15 – *"If you love Me, keep My commandments."*

6.) ASK *What stood out to most to you from those verses?* (2 or 3 popcorn answers)

Teaching

Knowing we need to be sanctified is the easy part; walking the walk is obviously harder.

7.) ASK *If we are honest with ourselves, what are some of the reasons we struggle to pursue holiness? What obstacles are in your way? How can we overcome them?* (2 or 3 popcorn answers)

Teaching

Remember that sanctification is a lifelong process, so we are working on this daily. This means we should not beat ourselves up as we stumble, but simply be quick to confess our sins and try again.

The **STEP OF SIMEON** was about *beginning* the path of obedience and daily confession. The **STEP OF NAPHTALI** is about *establishing* a Habit of Long Obedience.

8.) ASK *What are some techniques/habits you can begin to help you stay on course pursuing obedience daily?*

(4 or 5 popcorn answers – This is the most important question of the session, spend a little more time here.)

LEADER'S NOTE: As group leader, you should guide the discussion by elevating healthy practices and gently steering away from unhealthy answers. Two great practices are to make it a practice to ask God daily how we can obey Him better and/or to set up a visual cue in our homes to remind us to pursue obedience. Our Action Step this week is going to involve asking group members to set up such as visual cue in their home.

Teaching

Let's remember in the **STEP OF REUBEN**, we committed to make the Kingdom of God and its righteousness the top priority in our lives. **Let's recommit to this now!**

In Matthew 6:33, Jesus said, *"But seek first the Kingdom of God and His righteousness, and all these things shall be added to you."*

Therefore, Jesus is promising that if we make a priority of pursuing His holiness, He will provide for us and bless us with His favor.

We recognize this pursuit of obedience is and will be a daily struggle, which is why it is the STEP OF NAPHTALI, is "your struggle" and "my struggle."

Beyond re-committing to seek God's Kingdom as a top priority, a great practice is to make it a part of your daily prayer to ask God what He wants you to learn, where you need to obey Him better.

Some good questions to ask Him (among others) are:

- How can I follow you better?
- What do I need to understand?
- How can I show love to so-and-so better?
- Is there any place I need to obey You better?
- Where do I need to grow?
- How can I overcome this problem/bad habit?

Another recommendation is to set up a visual cue in a prominent place somewhere in your house that will remind you to be pursuing holiness daily. This is something God actually commanded the people of Israel to do:

Deuteronomy 6:4-9 – *"Hear, O Israel: The Lord our God, the Lord is one. Love the Lord your God with all your heart and with all your soul* *and with all your strength. These commandments that I give you today are to be on your hearts. Impress them on your children. Talk about them when you sit at home and when you walk along the road, when you lie down and when you get up. Tie them as symbols on your hands and bind them on your foreheads. Write them on the doorframes of your houses and on your gates.*

Today, many Jewish homes have something called a *Mezuzah* installed on their door posts, a small cylinder that contains a rolled-up scroll with the words of Deuteronomy 6:4-9 written on it. This is serves as a daily visual reminder to them of the importance of God's Word to them and the need to obey it.

So, we are recommending that you do the same thing! Not necessarily a *mezuzah* – it doesn't matter so much what the object is, it should just be something that will mean something to you and remind you. And it also doesn't have to be a permanently placed object. You could even just move a painting from one wall to another and every time you see it, you are reminded.

The Step of Naphtali is about establishing a Habit of Long Obedience in a believer's life.

Homework & Action Steps (5 min)

ASSIGN the homework for the coming week! Ask each member to try to complete the following before the next meeting:

Action Steps

COMMIT to pursuing obedience as a daily practice going forward.

BEGIN asking God in prayer every day to show you where you need to grow more like Jesus.

SET UP a visual cue in your home to remind you of your commitment to long obedience.

Homework

We all have a habitual sin we struggle to overcome. This week work to make significant progress in overcoming it through prayer and relying on God's power to overcome it.

Prayer (10-15 min)

Take a moment to pray for one another. Ask for any major prayer requests and ask certain members of the group to pray for others.

Repeat the requests slowly so everyone hears and those praying aren't embarrassed in the middle of their prayer by forgetting something.

(NOTE: 3 - 4 prayer requests is an ideal number. More than that can be overwhelming for the group to keep up with.)

STEP 7

GAD - גד

"A Cutting That Brings a Blessing"

THE WEAKNESS WE ARE STRENGTHENING

Many Christians are dominated by physical desires and are saturated with the world's influence. This lesson will help them learn to conquer their physical bodies and to turn off the world.

FOCUS

Beginning to fast and reduce the world's influence.

KEY VERSE

And do not be conformed to this world, but be transformed by the renewing of your mind, that you may prove what is that good and acceptable and perfect will of God.
(Romans 12:2)

KEY POINTS

- Jesus gave up ALL for *us* so we must be willing to give up ALL for *Him*. To follow Jesus means to imitate Him.
- The word "World" as we are referring to it in this lesson does not mean the physical earth, planets or even life. It means the current order of things, the culture that surrounds men and women.
- As Christians, we need to cut off any influences on our minds that are hurting our relationship with Christ.
- FASTING is an avenue that we can use to help reduce the World's influence.

The Step of Gad is about beginning a practice of fasting and being willing to sacrifice things of the world distracting us from the Kingdom.

The Study

Review (5 – 10 min)

REMIND about the **Step of Naphtali**, i.e., establishing a Habit of Long Obedience.

1.) Did everyone remember to set up a visual cue in their home to remind them to pursue obedience?

2.) Who would like to share about a new success in their pursuit of obedience this last week?

Ice Breaker (20 min)

ASK *What is your favorite TV Show and/or Movie and why do you like it?* (Everyone answers, in a circle)

Group Discussion (50 min)

LEADER'S NOTE: In this lesson, we are going to be inviting group members to begin practices of fasting and cutting off any influences on their mind that are hurting their relationship with Christ.

As the group leader, you should not be legalistic about this. Nor should you be issuing any specific commands as to what is okay culturally or not. (Of course, certain things like abortion, drug abuse, and sex trafficking are beyond dispute – we are more referring to specific movie & television choices for example.)

Instead, as group leader, late in the lesson, you should invite group members to pray about entertainment choices and see what God might say to them and invite them to join you in a fast which will also be described later in the lesson.

Teaching

The SEVENTH Step in the Path 2 Strength is the **Step of Gad**.

In most study Bibles, the name of Israel's seventh son, Gad, is translated in the footnotes as "troop." This is a simplified translation that prevents us from seeing the deeper meaning behind the name.

In fact, "troop" is actually an incorrect translation into English because it implies soldiers, or troops. A much better translation would be "raiders" or "bandits." The image the word conveys is a group of raiders that race their horses into a village, *cutting through it,* in order to retrieve its treasure.

Other ancient Hebrew uses of the word *gad* are when pagan priests would cut themselves to produce blood, or when a river would cut through a bank to reveal mineral deposits.

Thus, the true root meaning behind the name Gad is "a cutting that brings a blessing."

3.) **ASK** *What does this definition "a cutting that brings a blessing" make you think of?* (2-3 popcorn answers)

4.) **ASK** *Can you think of any personal sacrifice you've made in life that you would classify as a "Gad" act, i.e., a sacrifice that produced a blessing?* (2-3 popcorn answers)

5.) **ASK** *Obviously, Jesus dying for us on the cross was the* **ultimate** *Gad act. He sacrificed Himself so we could have the blessing of Heaven and eternal life with Him. What other "Gad" type acts did Jesus do for us?* (2-3 popcorn answers)

LEADER'S NOTE: Jesus gave up His heavenly power and position to be with us here on earth. He gave up peace and pure fellowship with the Father to live a life like one of us, suffering every temptation like us. He gave up riches to live like a poor man. He sacrificed constant obedience from angels to spend time teaching rebellious humans. He even gave up His reputation and subjected Himself to verbal abuse for our sakes.

Teaching

The name of Gad prophetically points to the ultimate cutting that produced a blessing, the Crucifixion of Christ on the Cross. His cutting allowed for our salvation which is priceless! This is the ultimate *Gad*!

We can also recognize many of the other things that Christ gave up for us. He gave up His throne in Heaven and all the power that came with it to humble Himself and live among us, suffering every hardship and temptation we endure. Then, He willingly gave up His very life to save us from a terrible destiny, redeeming us for eternity to Himself. (See Philippians 2:5-8)

Now, He calls us to follow Him, saying, *"And whoever does not bear his cross and come after Me cannot be My disciple."* (Luke 14:27)

To follow Him means to do as He did.
To imitate Him.

A big part of doing as He did is to give up anything we need to give up that is of this **World** *in order to follow Him.*

If He was willing to give up all for us, then we should be willing to give up all for Him.

6.) ASK *What does the word* ***"the World"*** *mean to you?* (2-3 popcorn answers)

Teaching

In the New Testament, the Greek word for "World" is *kosmos*, and the concept of *kosmos* in the Bible is bigger than we often understand.

Kosmos does not mean the physical earth, or the planet as we mean it, or even life. It means the current system, the current order of things. It refers to the collective systems and culture that govern men and women.

It is imperative that all Christians understand the full concept of this word "the World."

As the New Testament tells us, *"Do not be conformed to this world"* (Romans 12:2a), so we should understand that everything that is of the World is outside of and against the Kingdom of God.

7.) READ: Ask group members to read the following verses:

John 15:18-19 – *"If the world hates you, you know that it hated Me before it hated you. If you were of the world, the world would love its own. Yet because you are not of the world, but I chose you out of the world, therefore the world hates you."*

1 John 2:15 – *"Do not love the world or the things in the world. If anyone loves the world, the love of the Father is not in him."*

John 8:42-44a – *"Jesus said to them, 'If God were your Father, you would love Me, for I proceeded forth and came from God; nor have I come of Myself, but He sent Me. Why do you not understand My speech? Because you are not able to listen to My word. You are of your father the devil, and the desires of your father you want to do'."*

1 John 4:5 – *"They [non-believers] are of the world. Therefore, they speak as of the world, and the world hears them."*

John 17:16 – *"[Believers] are not of the world, just as I [Jesus] am not of the world."*

1 John 5:4 – *"For whatever is born of God overcomes the world. And this is the victory that has overcome the world—our faith."*

Teaching

Jesus is teaching us that there is a sharp difference between His teachings and the teachings of the World which originate with the devil.

Yet, many Christians try to live with feet in both the Kingdom and the World. They want to have citizenship in the Kingdom of

Christ, *but they don't want to give up their citizenship in the World either.*

8.) READ: Ask group members to read the following verses:

Luke 9:62 – *"But Jesus said to him, "No one, having put his hand to the plow, and looking back, is fit for the kingdom of God."*

James 4:4 – *"Adulterers and adulteresses! Do you not know that friendship with the world is enmity with God? Whoever therefore wants to be a friend of the world makes himself an enemy of God."*

Romans 12:2 – *"Do not be conformed to this World,* **but be transformed by the renewal of your mind,** *that by testing you may discern what is the will of God, what is good and acceptable and perfect."*

9.) ASK *Christians far too often let themselves be influenced by the beliefs and practices of the World. What are some of the beliefs of the World that you see influencing Christians that shouldn't?* (2-3 popcorn answers)

10.) ASK *Can you think of any television shows, movies, or other cultural influences that you could or should cut out of your life? How could this be a "Gad" act, "a cutting that produces a blessing"?* (2-3 popcorn answers)

Teaching

Fasting is the practice of forgoing food or other things for a set period of time for the purpose of seeking a closer walk with God or petitioning Him for something specific.

There are different kinds of fasts. The simplest kind is simply abstaining from food altogether for a few days drinking nothing more than water. Some might add juice to the fast. Others just abstain from sugar, desserts, or any good tasting foods for days or even weeks. And others may choose to give up other things like social media, television, or even sports.

The purpose of fasting is to declare to God that He is important to us, and that His Kingdom is important to us. It is also to show Him through action that something we are praying about is very important to us.

(Honestly, He already knows this, but it shows *us* whether something is truly important to us – if we are willing to give up food over it, then we definitely care about it!)

A secondary impact is that it helps us gain control over our flesh and its desires, or to reduce the importance and influence of the World over us.

Also, Jesus teaches us that fasting adds power to our prayers:

> *When Jesus saw that the people came running together, He rebuked the unclean spirit, saying to it, "Deaf and dumb spirit, I command you, come out of him and enter him no more!" Then, the spirit cried out, convulsed him greatly, and came out of him. And he became as one dead, so that many said, "He is dead." But Jesus took him by the hand and lifted him up, and he arose.*
>
> *And when He had come into the house, His disciples asked Him privately, "Why could we not cast it out?"*
>
> *So, He said to them, "This kind can come out by nothing but prayer and **fasting**."*
> *(Mark 9:14-29)*

11.) ASK *Have you ever participated in any kind of fast?* (2 or 3 popcorn answers)

As a group, we are going to attempt a simple 3-Day fast together over this next week!

<u>**Instructions**</u>

- Do not do anything that would jeopardize your health. Please take into account any special health conditions you may have.

- Decide what you are going to be personally fasting for? What are you going to be praying to God about?

- We are going to fast for 3 full days.

- The start time will be 72 hours before our next small group meeting time.

- We will break our fast together at the next meeting.

LEADER'S NOTE: You and your co-leaders should plan to have food ready for the group when they arrive at the next meeting. You can simply order pizza or some other food, or you can ask everyone to bring a dish and have a potluck.)

- Anyone who is overly intimidated by fasting for three full days can try starting with just one or two days.

- During the fast, remember why you are fasting. Every hunger pang is a reminder to pray.

LEADER'S NOTE: Leader, if someone in your group has a health condition like diabetes, please urge them to consult their doctor before fasting. Of course, they can also research fasting practices for their particular health condition online, but they should be participating at whatever level they feel is good for them without pressure from you.

- **Group members, you can do more than you think you can!** If you're not sure you can do the full three days, still push yourself to go a little bit past what you think you can. The result will be strong encouragement for yourself and new spiritual strength as you look back at what you just accomplished.

Teaching

When we meet again, we will talk about how our fast went and what we learned from it. In future weeks, you may choose to fast from other things for a time as well.

The Step of Gad is about learning how to fast and beginning to reduce the World's influence in a believer's life.

Homework & Action Steps (5 min)

MEMORIZE 1 John 2:15

"Do not love the world or the things in the world. If anyone loves the world, the love of the Father is not in him."

Action Steps

JOIN the group in a 3-Day Fast.

(**Leaders,** do everything in your power to fully participate in this fast yourself in order to set an example for them.)

Prayer (10-15 min)

Take a moment to pray for one another. Ask for any major prayer requests and ask certain members of the group to pray for others.

Repeat the requests slowly so everyone hears and those praying aren't embarrassed in the middle by forgetting something.

(NOTE: 3 - 4 prayer requests is an ideal number. More than that can be overwhelming for the group to keep up with.)

STEP 8

ASHER - אשר

"Happiness"

THE WEAKNESS WE ARE STRENGTHENING

Many Christians are exhausted and overwhelmed with life. They feel empty, like they never get a break, and they are not experiencing regular states of peace and joy. This lesson will help them learn to release their time to God, trusting Him, and enter into joy.

FOCUS

Beginning a regular Sabbath practice.

KEY VERSE

There remains therefore a rest for the people of God. For he who has entered His rest has himself also ceased from his works as God did from His. Let us therefore be diligent to enter that rest, lest anyone fall according to the same example of disobedience.
(Hebrews 4:9-11)

KEY POINTS

- Joy does not come from money or possessions.
- Obedience to God's Word and being close to His heart is the true path to joy.
- To observe the SABBATH is a command. It is not to annoy us but to free us up from all the cares of this world.
- Observing the Sabbath is STILL one of the Ten Commandments.
- By God's design our bodies/minds still need a day of rest.
- We should be asking how we can best honor God's intent on the Sabbath for rest and relationships.

The Step of Asher is about moving the Christian into a state of greater joy and peace, stronger relationships, and a deeper walk with God through regular and committed Sabbath practice.

Preparation

Group leaders, please prepare to have a feast waiting for your group when they arrive as a reward to celebrate the fast you all just achieved together! **You will break the fast together in fellowship.**

You, the group leader, *may* provide this meal for them, i.e., order pizza, home-cooked meal, or you can ask everyone to bring a dish and have more of a potluck dinner together. It is up to you.

The Study

Review (5 – 10 min)

REMIND about the **Step of Gad**, i.e., reducing the world's influence over us through sacrificing worldly things.

1.) **ASK** *How did your fast go?* (Discuss as a group everyone's successes or obstacles during the fast.)

Ice Breaker (20 min)

ASK *What would be your dream vacation? Where would you go? How long would you stay?*

Group Discussion (50 min)

Teaching

The EIGHTH Step in the Path 2 Strength is the **Step of Asher.**

The name Asher means "happiness," so in this lesson, we are going to begin talking about moving into joy.

2.) **ASK** *What would you say is the difference between happiness and joy?* (2-3 popcorn answers)

LEADER'S NOTE: It is often said that happiness is based on the circumstances in one's life, but that joy is more powerful. Joy is an elation inspired by God's love and His promises, it remains with us even in the face of problems. *Happiness depends on circumstances, but joy is retained in spite of circumstances.*

3.) ASK *Most of us know that joy is named as part of the Fruit of the Spirit, but what about happiness? Deep down in your heart of hearts, do you feel God wants you to be happy?* (2-3 popcorn answers)

Teaching

When asked if God wants them to be happy, a lot of Christians will tepidly answer "yes." Yet, if we are honest with ourselves, this is often only a head belief. It's something we believe intellectually because we think it is what we are supposed to say or believe, but we aren't necessarily convinced of it in our heart. We often have a lot of suspicion about whether or not God really wants us to be "happy."

Now, some Christians *do* passionately believe God wants them to be happy, but the rest of their beliefs aren't so biblical. Many are really worshipping a version of a fertility God instead of the God of the Bible. They believe "an abundant life" means God wants them to just increase their faith so He can give them health, wealth and/or other blessings.

Yet, God knows that joy does not come from possessions. *It comes from healthy spiritual living, from an intimate relationship with Him, and through loving relationships with others.*

Therefore, if we truly believe He wants to bless us with joy/happiness, we should seek greater obedience to His Word. If we trust in His heart for us, then we should also trust that His teachings, when followed, are what will actually lead us to joy.

Naturally, when a Christian is living in joy, they continue to feel a happiness even in the face of challenges. Joy is a deeper level of happiness that overcomes the world. So, pursuing joy should be a strong desire for us!

We don't have to look far to see the results of going the other way. Those politicians who grasp and hold onto power, do they seem to be happy and at peace? Or do they often seem embittered and short of temper?

A-list Hollywood stars achieve success, riches, fame, and adoration, yet behind the scenes, their personal lives are too often revealed to be empty and full of brokenness. Fake relationships, divorces, suicides, and addictions to alcohol and drugs are tragically abundant. Hollywood is not known as a place of sincerity, joy or peace.

It may surprise you, but in the business world, if one spends time with many of the top CEOs, one will not generally find sage leaders in possession of supreme wisdom for life, but men and women who sense a fragility and emptiness in their personal and spiritual lives. Many live in fear of illness and death because they don't have real answers to the most basic spiritual questions.

Whether we look to the political realm, to professional sports, to the entertainment industry, or the heads of large corporations, we don't find content people who have mastered life.

4.) READ: Ask several group members to read the following verses:

John 10:10 – *"The thief does not come except to steal, and to kill, and to destroy. I have come that they may have life, and that they may have it more abundantly."*

Galatians 5:22-23 – *"But the fruit of the Spirit is love, **JOY**, peace, longsuffering, kindness, goodness, faithfulness, gentleness, self-control. Against such there is no law."*

Teaching

Joy cannot be found in riches, fame, or success.

5.) READ: Ask a group member to read the following verse:

> *How can a young man cleanse his way?*
> *By taking heed according to Your word.*
> *With my whole heart I have sought You;*
> *Oh, let me not wander from Your commandments!*
> *Your word I have hidden in my heart,*
> *That I might not sin against You.*
> *Blessed are You, O Lord!*
> *Teach me Your statutes.*
> *With my lips I have declared*
> *All the judgments of Your mouth.*
> *I have rejoiced in the way of Your testimonies,*
> *As much as in all riches.*
> *I will meditate on Your precepts,*
> *And contemplate Your ways.*
> *I will delight myself in Your statutes;*
> *I will not forget Your word.*
> (Psalm 119:9-16)

Teaching

Obedience to God's Word and being close to His heart are the true path to joy.

And when it comes to experiencing an abundant life, God gives us a specific instruction designed to increase our happiness..

It's in Exodus 20, and we call it the Fourth Commandment:

6.) READ: Ask a group member to read Exodus 20:8-11:

> *Remember the Sabbath day, to keep it holy. Six days you shall labor and do all your work, but the seventh day is the Sabbath of the Lord your God. In it you shall do no work: you, nor your son, nor your daughter, nor your male servant, nor your female servant, nor your cattle, nor your stranger who is within your gates.* ***For in six days the Lord made the heavens and the earth, the sea, and all that is in them, and rested the seventh day. Therefore, the Lord blessed the Sabbath day and hallowed it.***

Teaching

The command to observe the Sabbath was not given to be an annoyance to us. It was given to free us up from all the cares of this world for an entire day every week!

Doesn't that actually sound nice?

What if God was trying to mandate a mini-vacation for us every week but we've been resisting it?

7.) ASK *What do you feel are some of the reasons people don't observe the Sabbath well?* (2-3 popcorn answers)

8.) ASK *What do you feel could be some of the benefits to observing the Sabbath regularly?* (2-3 popcorn answers)

Teaching

The Sabbath has many benefits for us.

The Sabbath gives our bodies rest. God did not design our bodies to work 24/7. Our need for sleep **every night** is clear, indisputable evidence God designed our bodies to have cycles of work and rest. Through the 4th Commandment, He is telling us that our bodies need a full day of rest once per week as well.

The Sabbath gives our minds rest. A healthy Sabbath is when we not only rest from physical labor, but we turn off all of our "work problems" mentally. We decide that all our anxieties and concerns can wait until the work week begins again. *It is a time to not even think about work or what we have to get done.*

Nothing has to get done on the Sabbath, so we can mentally rest.

The Sabbath is a tithe of our time. It is a declaration to God that He is the owner of our time. He is King and we follow His command about how best to use our time. The Sabbath is His, it is holy (meaning "set apart") for His special purposes.

To not observe a Sabbath is to refuse to acknowledge Him as Lord of Our Calendar. Through this choice, we are either saying we wish to remain the gods of our own calendar, or at a minimum we are saying we don't trust Him with our calendar.

NOTE: It is not so important *which* day of the week one celebrates the Sabbath as much as just making sure we have a regular one that interrupts our calendar. (For confirmation of this principle, see Romans 14:15). For most Christians, Sunday makes the most sense because of church services, etc. However, hospitals and certain other emergency services have to have employees work on Sundays, so some Christians may need to choose another day. Pastors themselves often choose a different day because they work all day every Sunday.

However, whatever day we honor as our Sabbath, we should not move it around from week to week at our convenience. **The Sabbath should be fixed for us and interrupt our calendar.** This is part of what it means to make God the Lord of our Calendar.

For those who might argue that the Sabbath is a part of the Old Testament Law which we are no longer under . . . we should recall the previous lessons where we've learned that those redeemed by Christ are simply no longer under the *penalty of death* for violating the Sabbath.

Our bodies' physical requirements have not changed. We still need a Sabbath day of rest every week *by His design*, and it still remains one of the Ten Commandments.

Christians typically don't question any of the other Ten Commandments as necessary for obedience to God. Yet, for some reason the Sabbath Day is frequently singled out as no longer relevant.

The reason for this is probably the multiple conflicts Jesus had with the Pharisees over healing on the Sabbath, but He initiated these conflicts not to abolish the Sabbath, but simply to show us that the

Sabbath was created for our blessing, not to be interpreted so legalistically as to become a curse.

LEADER'S NOTE: Some group members may ask about certain activities and whether they couldn't be an acceptable use of time on the Sabbath. For example, they may say "I enjoy yard work and feel like I'm spending time with God when I do it." The answer to this is that how they end up choosing to spend their Sabbath is between them and God. (The purpose of this course is not to dictate legalistic rules to follow.) Instead, they should simply be sure to sincerely ask themselves, "Am I trying to justify a certain activity on the Sabbath because I just really want to do it? Or am I sincerely allowing God to interrupt my calendar and this activity would truly help me spend more time with Him?" The answer to those questions will help the Christian navigate every situation.

Or a group member may say something like, "For me, shopping is fun, and I enjoy it!" This may be, but the Sabbath is not about personal fun. And those family members you take shopping with you may not enjoy it the same way you do. The Sabbath is about *resting*, not securing goods to meet personal needs which is to advance one's life forward. It's about spending time in relationships with God and others, which can include family fun, but should not be focused on personal entertainment.

The Sabbath gives us time for Worship! This mental and physical break from our work and busyness has a purpose of setting aside time for us to spend with God and worship Him. It is necessary for the continual growth of our relationship with Him.

The Sabbath gives us time to focus on relationships. Our work weeks are so filled with crazy levels of busyness, from work, to school, to sports, to every social obligation under the sun, the Sabbath provides a perfect break to slow down and really focus on time with family and friends.

The ideal Sabbath observance is one where it is kept on the same day every week, and the Christian fully rests from all work, all school studies, and *anything else that might help advance their life forward.*

Things to rest from would typically include most yard work, Children's sports activities, and even most shopping. These are all usually "have-to" activities that keep us busy and away from true rest.

9.) ASK *What aspect of the Sabbath observance would be the most challenging for you? (4 to 5 popcorn answers – Spend more time on this question.)*

LEADER'S NOTE: Some group members may have objections here that they will need to work through. Continue to emphasize the details remain between them and God.

Again, The purpose of this course is not to dictate legalistic rules to follow.

Instead, we simply should be asking ourselves, "Am I trying to approve a certain activity on the Sabbath because I just really want to do it? Or am I sincerely allowing God to interrupt my calendar and this activity would truly help me spend more time with Him?"

The answer to those questions will help the Christian navigate every situation.

10.) ASK *Would observing the Sabbath in the way God intended increase or decrease your happiness and how? (2 to 3 popcorn answers.)*

Teaching

In general, rather than trying to think of activities that could be "approved" or "excused" for the Sabbath (this is a legalistic approach), we should simply be asking how we can best honor God's intent on the Sabbath for rest and relationships.

The Sabbath is not about what "can" I do, it's about what "should" I do.

Does your Sabbath day look different from the rest of your days?

You know you are observing the Sabbath correctly if it looks different from the rest of the days of the week, you are able to spend time with God, and you feel rested at the end.

The Step of Asher is about moving the Christian into a state of greater joy and peace, stronger relationships, and a deeper walk with God through regular and committed Sabbath practice.

Homework & Action Steps (5 min)

REMIND that the Saturday following the next group meeting (Lesson 9) will be the neighborhood outreach! The location and more details will be discussed at the next meeting.

ASSIGN homework. Group members should watch as many of the Street Team training videos on the Path2Hope website in preparation of the outreach. (They are each about 5 minutes long; there are 12 total.)

Action Steps

COMMIT to observing the Sabbath in a biblical way going forward.

Prayer (10-15 min)

Take a moment to pray for one another. Ask for any major prayer requests and ask certain members of the group to pray for others.

Repeat the requests slowly so everyone hears and those praying aren't embarrassed in the middle of their prayer by forgetting something.

(NOTE: 3 - 4 prayer requests is an ideal number. More than that can be overwhelming for the group to keep up with.)

STEP 9

Issachar - יששכר

"He is hired"

LEADER'S NOTES

Welcome to Week 9!

This is the week we help the group step outside of their comfort zone and engage their neighbors in a positive way for the Kingdom!

Hopefully you have already been talking to your group about saving the date for the street outreach for several weeks now, if not since the beginning of the course.

Serving God with our energy and time is an important part of Kingdom Life. It's key to getting inactive Christians off the bench and working out their faith!

The name of Israel's ninth son, Issachar, means "He is hired," so this lesson is focusing on being "hired" by God and getting into the community to do His work.

Path2Hope Ministries has developed a very successful model for doing neighborhood outreach that is both easy and fun! With the Path2Hope method, typically, group members will get to have a good conversation with around 80% of the people who open doors to talk.

Hopefully you and your group members will have watched all the Street Team training videos on the Path2Hope website by the time of the outreach. If not, it's okay! **As long as you, the team leader, are familiar with the basic method Path2Hope uses, you can provide brief training the morning of the outreach event before going** out. (As needed, Path2Hope may/can send a representative to help with the training the morning of the event.)

Of course, experience shows that the more familiar you and your team members are with the Path2Hope principles, the more successful you will be!

IMPORTANT: Please know that, until they have participated for the first time, your group members will have a vague anxiety and dread about participating. Usually, it will be because of one or more of the following reasons:

- They worry they won't know what to say
- They think people will be annoyed/won't want to talk
- They think it will be boring/pointless
- They worry it might be unsafe

You, as group leader, should help them realize (as passionately as possible) that none of these things are true. Here are the best points to share BEFOREHAND to help persuade them to take a chance on stepping out:

They worry they won't know what to say.

Path2Hope has created easy to follow training videos on its website that will more than equip them for the outreach so they will know what to do and say. Anyone who comes to the outreach without having watched the videos can be trained within 20-30 minutes by someone who has.

The Path2Hope method is simple, easy and engaging.

They think people will be annoyed/won't want to talk.

Path2Hope has launched many Street Teams over the years, and we have never had any volunteer describe a neighborhood outreach with any word other than **"FUN"**!

The Path2Hope method does not involve "telling" people what to believe. It is showing a genuine, loving interest in people and trying to get to know them while inviting them into community.

The result is an 80% success rate in getting good conversations going with people who answer the door.

They worry it might be unsafe.

In the Path2Hope method, teams going door-to-door will always have 3 - 4 people per group, and each group will have a mixture of male and female. We also ask all group members to stay together until the outreach is finished. Generally, security is not a real problem, but these policies eliminate any issue that could arise.

They think it will be boring/pointless.

As before, all Path2Hope volunteers commonly describe participating in an outreach as "fun."

These outreaches are also not pointless, as we have seen many broken people accept Christ and begin fellowshipping in a local church because a Path2Hope Street Team came to their door.

THE METHOD:

The Path2Hope method is fairly simple. Rather than "telling" people what to believe, **we knock on doors offering food and prayer** in an inviting way. **We ask a lot of questions** in a genuine effort to get to know them. **And we are sure to make a formal invitation** of some kind, to accept Christ, or to attend a church service.

WHERE TO GO:

Your group is free to choose the location of the outreach! Of course, Path2Hope stands ready to offer counsel and recommend locations near you that seem promising.

Path2Hope strongly recommends doing outreach in lower-income neighborhoods rather than middle class neighborhoods. This ensures the greatest success.

The reason is that people experiencing a greater level of brokenness or poverty are typically more open to the Gospel and an outreach team. In a middle-class neighborhood, people do not perceive their own need as greatly and are less open to conversation.

So, how then do we reach middle-class or wealthy people?

Participating in a Path2Hope outreach has TWO benefits. Not only do we reach people during the outreach with the Gospel, but team members learn how to start spiritual conversations and answer many questions. This "breaks the ice" so to speak for them and allows them to go back into their own neighborhoods and work environment, sharing the Gospel one-on-one with family, friends, and co-workers.

Path2Hope outreaches are training grounds for greater personal ministry!

WHEN **TO GO:**

For the first outreach, Path2Hope recommends going on a Saturday morning. First-time participants should meet at fast-food restaurant or donut shop at 9:00 am for training. You and/or a Path2Hope representative will provide brief training at that time.

Then, at around 10:00 am, the team prays and travels to the chosen neighborhood and begins knocking on doors. Usually, teams do this for about two hours until 12:00 pm (noon)!

After the first outreach, your team is free to choose future times and locations that work best for your members!

(We do not recommend doing outreach after dark.)

FOLLOW-UP:

As team leader, please make sure your team members are taking note of the names, phone numbers, and prayer requests of the people they talk to. This is so Path2Hope staff members can reach out to them afterward and keep reaching them spiritually.

There are three important things to do to make sure this happens well:

1.) **Group members should be sure to mention they are with the ministry Path2Hope** at some point during the conversation. (This is so the individual is not surprised when a staff member from Path2Hope follows-up with them.)

2.) **At the end of the conversation, simply ask, "Hey, do you mind if we get your phone number so we can follow up with you?"** Usually, people have no problem providing this AFTER a good conversation.

3.) **Be sure to upload your data!** The easiest way to do this is to have group members entering and submitting the data as they go through the form on the Path2Hope website. If not, please be sure to get all the names and phone numbers and requests from each group before they go home and then email it to Path2Hope for processing.

Path2Hope staff will contact all those reached, especially those with physical or spiritual needs. Path2Hope will attempt to help individuals connect with local ministries and services that can meet physical needs, and we will offer mentoring and connect them to local churches for spiritual needs.

THE FUTURE:

It is hoped that your group will decide to form a permanent outreach team that goes out at least once per month going forward, even as the small group moves on to study other things!

Outreach Teams usually follow the small group semester system. They break from December – February and from June - July.

The Step of Issachar is about getting the Christian off the bench and serving. In order to assist this, Path2Hope has created Outreach Teams as a way to get believers more connected with their community.

The Weakness We Are Strengthening

Many Christians are inactive and not helping expand the Kingdom of God, which is one of the main purposes for Christians on earth. This step helps activate Christians and get them into the community.

Focus

Beginning to serve in the Kingdom.

Key Verse

*Never be lacking in zeal, but keep
your spiritual fervor, serving the Lord.*
(Romans 12:11)

Key Points

- God wants to HIRE us for work in His fields.
- Everyone is given spiritual gifts to empower them to serve God better. We are to use our gifts together as one body to glorify God.
- Outreach Teams from Path2Hope are Body-Building Teams, designed to provide an opportunity for ALL to use their gifts together to build the body of Christ.
- Path2Hope has training videos available to help prepare oneself before going on an outreach.
- Outreaches are FUN!

The Study

SPECIAL PREPARTION: The host should have a TV available with HDMI connection. Some of the Path2Hope training videos will be shown during this lesson.

The easiest way is to play them on a laptop from the Path2Hope website and change the input on the TV to match the laptop screen.

Review (5 – 10 min)

REMIND about the **STEP OF ASHER**, i.e., moving into joy and more rest as we make declare God to be Lord of our Time by observing the Sabbath.

1.) **ASK** *How did your Sabbath go?* (Discuss as a group everyone's successes or obstacles from the fast the previous week.)

Ice Breaker (20 min)

ASK *If you could have any job in the world at all and make a good living doing it, what would your favorite job be?*

Group Discussion (50 min)

2.) **ASK** *How do you feel your country is doing today? How are the people doing? Are there serious problems? Or is everything okay?* ***What kinds of problems do you see?*** (2-3 popcorn answers)

LEADER'S NOTE: Let the group talk a moment about the state of the country (generally not good). Let the weight of the darkness surrounding us set in for a moment.

3.) ASK *Do you think the government can solve these problems? What about the Church? Can these problems be solved without the Church engaging society and making a difference?* (2-3 popcorn answers)

LEADER'S NOTE: The obvious answer is no, the government cannot solve these problems or they would have already. Only the Church can make a difference. The next question then is *who* is the Church.

4.) ASK the group to THNK SILENTLY for a moment about *Are you part of the Church that needs to engage society?* (2-3 popcorn answers)

LEADER"S NOTE: The purpose of the sequence of questions above is to help each group member come to the realization that it is *they* who must step out to make a difference in our nation and community, not someone else.

Teaching

The NINTH Step in the Path 2 Strength is the **STEP OF ISSACHAR.**

The name Issachar means "He is hired." *God wants to hire you for work in His fields!*

So, in this lesson, we are talking about serving God through ministry to others.

5.) READ: Ask several group members to read the following verses:

Matthew 9:36-38 – *"But when He saw the multitudes, He [Jesus] was moved with compassion for them, because they were weary and scattered, like sheep having no shepherd. Then He said to His disciples, "The harvest truly is plentiful, but the laborers are few. Therefore, pray the Lord of the harvest to send out laborers into His harvest."*

1 Corinthians 15:58 – *"Therefore, my beloved brethren, be steadfast, immovable, always abounding in the work of the Lord, knowing that your labor is not in vain in the Lord."*

Romans 12:10-11 – *"Be kindly affectionate to one another with brotherly love, in honor giving preference to one another; not lagging in diligence, fervent in spirit, serving the Lord."*

Joshua 24:15 – *"And if it seems evil to you to serve the Lord, choose for yourselves this day whom you will serve, whether the gods which your fathers served that were on the other side of the River, or the gods of the Amorites, in whose land you dwell. But as for me and my house, we will serve the Lord."*

Hebrews 6:10 – *"For God is not unjust to forget your work and labor of love which you have shown toward His name, in that you have ministered to the saints, and do minister."*

6.) ASK *What are some of the different ways Christians can serve God? How have you seen Christians serving God?* (2-3 popcorn answers)

LEADER' NOTE: We would like the group to discuss all kinds of serving options here. From ushering to children's ministry to food pantries and worship, there are many ways to serve God. **Group leader, feel free to invite your pastor or missions/outreach pastor to visit your group this week to speak briefly about the different service opportunities at your church.**

Teaching

The Bible teaches that the Holy Spirit gives all Christians special spiritual gifts to empower them to serve Him better. Every Christians is given a different combination of gifts, and these gifts are supposed to be used together, meaning we work together with our gifts as one body to glorify God.

The Bible also teaches that no gift is better or more important than another.

7.) READ: Ask group members to read the following verses:

1 Corinthians 12:1-11 – *"Now concerning spiritual gifts, brethren, I do not want you to be ignorant: You know that you were Gentiles,* carried away to these dumb idols, however you were led. Therefore, I make known to you that no one speaking by the Spirit of God calls Jesus accursed, and no one can say that Jesus is Lord except by the Holy Spirit.

There are diversities of gifts, but the same Spirit. There are differences of ministries, but the same Lord. And there are diversities of activities, but it is the same God who works all in all. But the manifestation of the Spirit is given to each one for the profit of all: for to one is given the **word of wisdom** through the Spirit, to another the **word of knowledge** through the same Spirit, to another **faith** by the same Spirit, to another **gifts of healings** by the same Spirit, to another the **working of miracles**, to another **prophecy**, to another **discerning of spirits**, to another **different kinds of tongues**, to another the **interpretation of tongues**. But one and the same Spirit works all these things, distributing to each one individually as He wills.

1 Corinthians 12:12-31 – *"For as the body is one and has many members, but all the members of that one body, being many, are one body, so also is Christ. For by one Spirit we were all baptized into one body—whether Jews or Greeks, whether slaves or free—and have all been made to drink into one Spirit. For in fact the body is not one member but many.*

If the foot should say, "Because I am not a hand, I am not of the body," is it therefore not of the body? And if the ear should say, "Because I am not an eye, I am not of the body," is it therefore not of the body? If the whole body were an eye, where would be the hearing? If the whole were hearing, where would be the smelling? But now God has set the members, each one of them, in the body just as He pleased. And if they were all one member, where would the body be?

But now indeed there are many members, yet one body. And the eye cannot say to the hand, "I have no need of you"; nor again the head to the feet, "I have no need of you." No, much rather, those members of the body which seem to be weaker are necessary. And those members of the body which we think to be less honorable, on these we bestow greater honor; and our unpresentable parts have greater modesty, but our presentable parts have no need. But God composed the body, having given greater honor to that part which lacks it, that there should be no schism in the body, but that the members should have the same care for one another. And if one member suffers, all the members suffer with it; or if one member is honored, all the members rejoice with it.

Now you are the body of Christ, and members individually. And God has appointed these in the church: **first apostles, second prophets, third teachers, after that, miracles, then gifts of healings, helps, administrations, varieties of tongues.** *Are all apostles? Are all prophets? Are all teachers? Are all workers of miracles? Do all have gifts of healings? Do all speak with tongues? Do all interpret? But earnestly desire the best gifts. And yet I show you a more excellent way."*

8.) **ASK** *Do you know what your spiritual gifts are? Have you ever taken a spiritual gifts test?* (Everyone answer in a circle.)

Teaching

If you aren't sure what your spiritual gifts are, just google "spiritual gifts test" and you will find several links for online tests. Path2Hope recommends taking 2-3 tests to see which gifts show up as consistently strong between them all.

The outreach teams that Path2Hope has developed are not evangelism teams, or prayer teams, they are **Body-Building Teams.** *This means they are designed to provide an opportunity for all of the gifts to be used together to build the Body of Christ.*

Some people use their gift of evangelism or teaching when speaking with people. Others are prayer warriors who are praying for the conversations as they are happening. Others have the gift of mercy and are looking for ways they and Path2Hope can help meet the physical needs of people struggling, and still other may be gifted in administration and can help organize the team and make it go.

This Saturday, we are going to be doing our first outreach! We are going to meet at _____ (location) at 9 AM for prayer and training, and it's going to be a lot of fun!

9.) **SAY** *It is common for people to feel nervous before their first time. Do **you** feel any anxiety about going out? Any concerns? If so, what are they?* (2-3 popcorn answers)

Teaching

(If group members seem to have a higher level of worry about the outreach, spend a little more time on this part of the teaching. If not, you can mention the points below fairly quickly and move on.)

For those that worry they won't know what to say:

Path2Hope has created easy to follow training videos on its website that will more than equip you for the outreach so you will know what to do and say. Anyone who comes to the outreach without having watched the videos can be trained within 20-30 minutes by someone who has.

The Path2Hope method is simple, easy and engaging.

For those that think people will be annoyed or won't want to talk:

Path2Hope has launched many Street Teams over the years and has rarely had any volunteer describe a neighborhood outreach with any word other than **"FUN"**!

The Path2Hope method does not involve "telling" people what to believe. It is about showing a genuine, loving interest in people and trying to get to know them while inviting them into community.

The result is an 80% success rate in getting good conversations going with people who answer the door.

11.) **WATCH** *the Street Team training video called "Going Door-to-Door" (ST Training 2)*

https://path2hope.org/street1/

12.) WATCH *the Street Team training called "Names Before Donuts" (ST Training 3)*

https://path2hope.org/street1/

13.) WATCH *the Street Team training called "Offering Prayer" (ST Training 4)*

https://path2hope.org/street2/

14.) ASK *Does anyone have any pressing questions about the outreach? (2 to 3 popcorn answers.)*

Teaching

Well, for anyone who hasn't watched the rest of the Path2Hope training videos, we strongly recommend doing so before the outreach! They're not very long and you will learn a lot!

If for some reason you can't, don't worry about it and still come! We will see you Saturday!

The Step of Issachar is about moving Christians off the bench and into the field!

Action Step

Neighborhood Outreach!

Prayer (10-15 min)

Take a moment to pray for one another. Ask for any major prayer requests and ask certain members of the group to pray for others.

Repeat the requests slowly so everyone hears and those praying aren't embarrassed in the middle of their prayer by forgetting something.

(NOTE: 3 - 4 prayer requests is an ideal number. More than that can be overwhelming for the group to keep up with.)

STEP 10

ZEBULUN - יששכר

"Glorious Dwelling Place"

LEADER'S NOTES

By now, you should be starting to see new strength and confidence in the faces of your group members!

Hopefully your team had a successful outreach the previous Saturday and everyone had a great experience. It is incredible how powerfully God moves during these outreaches.

The name Zebulun means "Glorious Dwelling Place," and it's a name that is pointing us toward our true home, Heaven.

So far, on the Path 2 Strength, we have made efforts to truly make God the Lord of our lives in the following ways:

Lord of Our Hearts	Obedience	(Naphtali)
Lord of Our Minds	Sanctification	(Gad)
Lord of Our Time	Sabbath	(Asher)
Lord of Our Energy	Service	(Issachar)

But there is one more area where we need to declare God to be the Lord. He is Lord of Our Money!

As Jesus said:

> *"Do not lay up for yourselves treasures on earth, where moth and rust destroy and where thieves break in and steal; but lay up for yourselves treasures in heaven, where neither moth nor rust destroys and where thieves do not break in and steal. For where your treasure is, there your heart will be also."*

(Matthew 6:19-21)

Jesus is clearly saying that storing up wealth here on earth is a worthless endeavor and that we should instead be using our wealth in generous ways to store up treasures for ourselves in Heaven.

His teaching makes it clear that there will be real rewards, *valuable* rewards given to us in Heaven according to our generosity here on earth.

So, if we believe the words of Jesus, we obey them. We learn to use our money for Kingdom advancement.

Because of this principle, the Step of Zebulun is about a faithful practice of the tithe as a starting point and making generous giving a way of life.

As the leader, you should know that this is one of the places where you might get significant pushback from one or more group members. This should not surprise you. As Jesus said, "Where your treasure is, there your heart is also." So, if you touch someone's pocketbook, they tend to get the most excited.

Pushback does not mean you have done something wrong, or taught wrong, because tithing is a clear biblical principle. It simply means you have touched a sensitive spot.

In this lesson, we will attempt to be as gentle as possible while clearly teaching the truth.

Some helpful things that can be said at some point during the discussion that can disarm many objections are:

- While it is best to give to the church you personally attend, it doesn't really matter to which church you tithe. We are not saying you have to give to any specific church, or any particular denomination; the principle is about giving to God, period.

- Tithing is an act of worship, not a donation.

- Tithing is a statement to God that you recognize Him as the source of all of your money and possessions, and you are rightfully giving Him the tribute due Him as King of Kings.

- It does not matter what your pastor or any other church leaders do with the money. That is between them and God. Whether or not *you* give sacrificially is what God is concerned about.

The Weakness We Are Strengthening

Many Christians do not live in a way that shows they recognize God as Lord of their wealth. Usually, fear, stinginess, or greed is the source of this.

Focus

Establishing a tithing habit. Moving into generosity.

Key Verse

For where your treasure is, there your heart will be also.
(Matthew 6:21)

Key Points

- A TITHE is "one tenth" or 10%. We tithe to honor God as our provider. It is an act of Worship!
- Tithing is a statement to God showing we recognize Him as the source of our wealth and provision.
- Tithing is having Faith in God to keep His promise. (Malachi 3:10)
- Jesus needs to be Lord of ALL of our life which includes our money.

The Step of Zebulun is about learning to worship God as the Lord of Our Wealth.

The Study

SPECIAL PREPARTION: The host should have a TV available with HDMI connection. Video will be shown during this lesson.

The easiest way is to play them on a laptop from the Path2Hope website and change the input on the TV to match the laptop screen.

Review (5 – 10 min)

REMIND about the **Step of Issachar**, i.e., the joy of serving God for His glory and the expansion of His Kingdom!

1.) ASK *So, how did everyone like the outreach? Any new thoughts since we went?*

Ice Breaker (20 min)

If money were no object, what crazy or unique thing would you love to have in your dream home?

Group Discussion (50 min)

2.) ASK *If we consider the average American **Christian**, what would you guess they spend more time thinking about: How to build their personal wealth or How to build the Kingdom of God? If you had to assign percentages, what percent of the time would you guess for each?* (2-3 popcorn answers)

3.) ASK *How real is Heaven to you? What do you think Heaven is going to be like? In your imagination, how is it?* (Give a little more time for this, 4-5 popcorn answers)

4.) WATCH *the Heaven compilation video called "Heaven Seen" (on the Path2Hope site)* https://path2hope.org/heavenseen/

Teaching

The TENTH Step in the Path 2 Strength is the **STEP OF ZEBULUN.**

The name Zebulun means "Glorious Dwelling Place."[1] It is an allusion to Heaven, the ultimate home of us believers!

4.) READ: Ask a group member to read Matthew 6:19-21:

"Do not lay up for yourselves treasures on earth, where moth and rust destroy and where thieves break in and steal; but lay up for yourselves treasures in heaven, where neither moth nor rust destroys and where thieves do not break in and steal. For where your treasure is, there your heart will be also."

5.) ASK *What does this passage mean to you? How actively are you working to store up treasure in Heaven?* (2-3 popcorn answers)

6.) READ: Ask group members to read the following verses:

Hebrews 7:1-4 – *"For this Melchizedek, king of Salem, priest of the Most High God, who met Abraham returning from the slaughter of the kings and blessed him, to whom also Abraham gave a tenth part of all, first being translated 'king of righteousness,' and then also king of Salem, meaning 'king of peace,' without father, without mother, without genealogy, having neither beginning of days nor end of life, but made like the Son of God . . . to whom even the patriarch **Abraham gave a tenth of the spoils.***

Proverbs 3:9-10 – *"Honor the Lord with your possessions, And with **the firstfruits** of all your increase; So your barns will be filled with plenty, And your vats will overflow with new wine."*

---

[1] https://www.abarim-publications.com/Meaning/Zebulun.html

Leviticus 27:30 – *"And all **the tithe** of the land, whether of the seed of the land or of the fruit of the tree, is the Lord's. It is holy to the Lord."*

Malachi 3:8-9 – *"Will a man rob God? Yet you have robbed Me! But you say, 'In what way have we robbed You?'* **In tithes and offerings.** *You are cursed with a curse, for you have robbed Me, even this whole nation.*

7.) ASK *What do you think are some of the different reasons some* ***Christians*** *don't tithe?* (2-3 popcorn answers)

Teaching

No matter how talented, how intelligent, or how strong someone is, they could not earn money without the body God gave them. Everyone who has a functioning brain, a mouth that works, and a stomach to digest their food, owes those things to Him. And if we are blessed to have two arms and legs, two eyes to see, and general health to live well, we should recognize those things are also from Him and usually needed to earn money. Not to mention the talents and gifts He's given each of us.

We did not choose the country into which we were born, He chose that for us. He is also the one who brought us the opportunities and resources that have come our way. He is the one who makes the sun to shine upon us all, who causes it to rain on every field, and who brings crops to harvest for us to eat.

Therefore, no one has ever earned a single penny without His help.

The tithe, which means "one tenth" or "10%," is the amount of our income we give back to God in order to honor Him as our provider. It is an act of worship, and Abraham modeled it for us almost 4,000 years ago.

Yet, many Christians don't practice a tithe regularly! Here are a few of the more common reasons:

A.) It's considered part of the Old Testament Law, not the New Testament.

Jesus did not do away with God's Law, He provided an escape from the *penalty* of breaking it. So, a Christian who doesn't tithe will no longer be penalized for it.

However, if our only reason for not tithing is we don't "have to" anymore, then can we truly call ourselves grateful to God for what He has done for us? How can a Christian whose beginning point is only doing what they have to do be considered generous and loving toward God?

B.) They don't like how their church is spending the money.

How a pastor, a priest, a board of elders or deacons, or the majority vote of a congregation decide to spend money donated to a church is between them and God.

When we give the tithe, *it is not a donation*. It is an act of worship!

As far as we are concerned, it honestly doesn't matter if a pastor takes the cash we've given out back and burns it. If such a thing were happening, you of course might want to seriously consider changing churches, but if you are not a part of the church's accountability/governing authority, then that is between the church and God.

Our responsibility is to give as an act of worship, period. We give the tithe as a statement to God that we recognize Him as the source of our wealth and provision. What happens to our gift after that is His problem, not ours.

C.) They are afraid they can't afford it.

This is a common fear, so if you struggle with it, you are not alone!

Yet, this is what God said to us through the prophet Malachi:

> *"Bring all the tithes into the storehouse,*
> *That there may be food in My house,*

> *And try Me now in this,"*
> *Says the Lord of hosts,*
> *"If I will not open for you the windows of heaven*
> *And pour out for you such blessing*
> *That there will not be room enough to receive it."*
> (Malachi 3:10)

Many Christians have experienced supernatural financial provision from God once they begin to tithe, and this is exactly what God is promising in Malachi 3. It isn't a "get-rich-quick" scheme kind of promise, but He is promising to take care of us financially if we trust Him enough to tithe.

This is faith. If we truly believe this promise of God, we will act on it in trust.

This is the *only* area in Scripture where God tells us it's okay to test Him on something. In fact, in this promise, He is inviting us to!

8.) ASK *Have you ever been generous with God and experienced a supernatural provision from Him afterward? If not, are you willing to test Him and try the promise of Malachi 3? (2-3 popcorn answers)*

Teaching

Money is a sensitive subject for many people. But if Jesus is Lord of our Life, He must be Lord of ALL of our Life, and that includes our money.

Just as it would be impossible to claim that Jesus is Lord of Our Calendar without giving Him any of our time, so it is impossible to claim that Jesus is Lord of Our Wallet if we don't give Him any of our money. It's that simple.

Why not take a chance?

If you haven't been tithing well, now is a great time to start! Let's take God up on His invitation to test Him and see what He does.

And if you have been tithing well, maybe it's time to consider if there are ways to support Kingdom work in a greater way and store up some more treasures in Heaven!

The Step of Zebulun is about the Christian truly making God the Lord of their Wealth!

Homework & Action Steps (5 min)

Action Steps

COMMIT to writing out a family budget if you don't have one already. COMMIT to attempting to tithe this week.

Prayer (10-15 min)

Take a moment to pray for one another. Ask for any major prayer requests and ask certain members of the group to pray for others.

Repeat the requests slowly so everyone hears and those praying aren't embarrassed in the middle of their prayer by forgetting something.

(NOTE: 3 - 4 prayer requests is an ideal number. More than that can be overwhelming for the group to keep up with.)

STEP 11

JOSEPH - יוֹסֵף

"Yahweh Adds"

LEADER'S NOTES

We have walked together a good way on the Path to Strength so far. To see where we have led the group up to this point, review the chart and explanations of the first 10 steps under "The Study" section of this lesson.

If a Christian sincerely accepts everything outlined in the first ten lessons and commits these principles to heart and practices them, they will experience a new Spiritual Confidence and Strength, and a Reinvigorated Walk with God. They will have laid down a strong foundation and begin to feel the abundant life and a clearer sense of purpose.

The last four steps, those of Joseph, Manasseh, Ephraim, and Benjamin are about moving into the fullness of spiritual strength and beginning to bear fruit. Some participants may be already prepared by God to bear much fruit. Others may be much younger and only produce a small amount of fruit at first.

We are not so concerned about how much fruit a Christian is bearing as much as whether or not they are continuing on the growth path.

In this week's session, we will help our group members see that it's actually not so hard to do that. It can be as easy as purposefully repeating to others some of the key principles we've learned in the Path2Strength course.

THE WEAKNESS WE ARE STRENGTHENING

Many Christians don't see themselves as teachers, as "disciple-makers." They don't feel they have the confidence or the strength or the knowledge to disciple others and may even feel it's not their role.

Focus

Beginning to disciple others.

Key Verse

Therefore, go and make disciples of all nations, baptizing them in the name of the Father and of the Son and of the Holy Spirit, and teaching them to obey everything I have commanded you. And surely I am with you always, to the very end of the age.
(Matthew 28:19-20)

Key Points

- God CALLS all of His followers to go and make disciples!
- 4 Steps to begin the discipleship process:
    A. COMMIT – Commit to God that you're open to the process.
    B. PRAY – Ask God to send you someone to disciple.
    C. LOOK – Be intentional in looking for someone to disciple.
    D. ASK – While conversing with others, ask "open" spiritual questions.

The Step of Joseph is about beginning to disciple others.

The Study

SPECIAL PREPARTION: Pass out copies of the Path2Strength feedback questionnaire and have group members fill them out before starting the group. The questionnaires are short, so the leader can allow about 10 minutes for this.

Please collect the questionnaires at the end and send scanned or mailed copies back to Path2Hope so we can continue to improve the course!

Review (5 – 10 min)

REMIND about the **STEP OF ZEBULUN**, i.e., worshipping God through the tithe.

1.) ASK *Did anyone have any breakthroughs this week with regard to tithing?*

Ice Breaker (20 min)

Tell us about someone in your life you feel God used more than most to bring you to Christ? (Go in a circle, everyone answers.)

Group Discussion (50 min)

2.) ASK *Since we've embarked on this journey together, do you feel stronger? How has your spiritual walk improved? (4 – 5 popcorn answers, spend a little more time on this.)*

Teaching

We have walked together a good way on the Path to Strength so far. Here is where we have gone as a group up to this point:

TRIBE	MEANING	STEP
REUBEN	*Behold, a Son*	Christ as Priority
SIMEON	*He Who Obeys*	Confess & Obey - Clear Relationship w/ God
LEVI	*My Joining*	Prayer Habit
JUDAH	*Praise*	Fellowship Habit
DAN	*Judge*	Bible Habit
NAPHTALI	*My Struggle*	Lord of Our Heart (Long Obedience)
GAD	*Sacrifice That Brings Blessing*	Lord of Our Mind (Sanctification from World)
ASHER	*Happiness*	Lord of Our Time (Observe the Sabbath)
ISSACHAR	*He is Hired*	Lord of Our Body (Serving God)
ZEBULUN	*Glorious Dwelling*	Lord of Our Money (Tithing Well)

The chart makes it self-evident why any believer would become stronger in their faith and relationship with God as they walk the Path 2 Strength.

The first two **STEPS OF REUBEN & SIMEON** are about re-orienting our life and mental focus to be centered around Jesus and then clearing the relationship with God by confessing any unconfessed sins and beginning to intentionally increase obedience.

The next three, the **STEPS OF LEVI, JUDAH, AND DAN** are about establishing the three foundational spiritual habits of Bible-reading, prayer and fellowship in a believer's life. Without all three of these habits, spiritual growth is not possible. With them, all things are possible.

The next five, **NAPHTALI, GAD, ASHER, ISSACHAR, AND ZEBULUN** are about progressively turning over to God a different part of our lives. If we make God the Lord of our Heart, our Mind, our Body, our Time, and our Money, what part of us could possibly remain outside His Lordship?

3.) ASK *How important do you think it is for Christians across America to understand these lessons?* (2-3 popcorn answers)

Teaching

If a Christian sincerely accepts everything outlined in the first ten lessons and commits these principles to heart and practices them, they will experience a new Spiritual Confidence and Strength, and a Reinvigorated Walk with God. They will have laid down a strong foundation, begin to feel the abundant life, and have a clearer sense of purpose.

The ELEVENTH Step in the Path 2 Strength is the **STEP OF JOSEPH.**

The name Joseph means "Yahweh adds," so this step is about discipleship. Specifically, you discipling others.

Does that thought intimidate you?

4.) ASK *Have you ever thought of yourself as a teacher? Do you see yourself as someone who influences others?* (2-3 popcorn answers)

5.) ASK *Do you think intentionally discipling others is something only some Christians should do? Or do you think it's a requirement for all believers?* (2-3 popcorn answers)

Teaching

Right before He ascended into Heaven, Jesus gave all His followers one last command. He said:

"Go therefore and make disciples of all the nations, baptizing them in the name of the Father and of the Son and of the Holy Spirit."
(Matthew 28:19)

As we are all aware, our country has some major spiritual and social problems that need to be fixed urgently. Our country's future doesn't look good if they aren't.

6.) ASK *Can our society's problems be fixed without discipleship? Who will do the discipling if you don't?* (1-2 popcorn answers, very brief discussion, this question is more for meditation and consideration.)

7.) READ: Ask group members to read the following verses:

2 Timothy 2:2 – *"You have heard me teach things that have been confirmed by many reliable witnesses. Now teach these truths to other trustworthy people who will be able to pass them on to others."* (NLT)

Luke 6:40 – *"A disciple is not above his teacher, but everyone who is perfectly trained will be like his teacher."*

Luke 9:23 – *"Then He said to them all, 'If anyone desires to come after Me, let him deny himself, and take up his cross daily, and follow Me.'"*

Matthew 10:37 – *"He who loves father or mother more than Me is not worthy of Me. And he who loves son or daughter more than Me is not worthy of Me."*

Teaching

So, Jesus tells us that *all* of us need to be discipling others. That the responsibility to do the work of redeeming our country and people by expanding the Kingdom of God lies with each of us, one disciple at a time.

Let's imagine a scenario with two Christians who want to disciple others:

Christian #1: Sometimes posts Bible verses on Facebook and makes the occasional comment on someone else's political post when it seems outrageous enough to warrant it. When they see friends or family posting/saying things that aren't very biblical, they resolve to pray harder for them and make a few finely crafted comments at family gatherings or parties in hopes it might plant a seed.

Christian #2: Looks around for struggling or lukewarm Christians to disciple. When they find someone who is teachable, they begin talking to them about the Step of Reuben. Then, over time, they try to intentionally walk them through each of the other steps of the **Path2Strength** in order.

8.) ASK *Which of the Christians above do you think would be more effective at making disciples for Christ? Why?* (2-3 popcorn answers)

Teaching

So, if we want to obey Jesus, we must commit to try to engage in discipleship.

Yet, we are immediately faced with an apparent obstacle. *Who am I going to disciple? How do I even get someone to let me disciple them?*

Here is how to begin the discipleship process in 4 easy steps:

- **A.) Commit.** Tell God in your heart that you are open and available to disciple others. Tell Him that you want to disciple others.

- **B.) Pray.** Ask God to send you someone to disciple. Decide to believe He will do it.

- **C.) Look.** Decide to be intentional about looking for the right people to teach.

- **D.) Ask.** Asking open spiritual questions is a great way to start a good conversation. A fantastic question that usually works pretty well is: *What is your relationship like with God right now?*

Many Christians will respond by admitting that it's not good, or they haven't heard from Him for a while, or they're struggling. If they say something along those lines, then they are *exactly* the kind of person **Path 2 Strength** was designed for.

If they say something like that, you can simply say, "*Hey, I've been going through this course called Path2Strength, and it's really helped me feel stronger and closer to God. That's what the whole course is about! Would you like me to begin sharing with you some of the things I've been learning there?*"

If they say, "no, not interested," then move on!

If they say, "yes, that sounds good," or something along those lines, you've got yourself a disciple!

You can either begin teaching them some about the **Step of Reuben** right then, or if pressed for time, you can discuss setting up a regular day/time per week to talk.

REMEMBER: Structure is very important for the discipleship process.

It is important to emphasize that there are various lessons you've learned and want to share. That each one will help them grow stronger, but they need to be learned in order. Yet, you are confident they will feel the impact of them transforming their Christian life.

9.) **ASK** *What are some other good "open" spiritual questions you could ask to start a conversation? (2 – 3 popcorn answers)*

10.) **ASK** *Do you have anyone in mind already you know that might be a discipleship candidate? (2 – 3 popcorn answers)*

Teaching

Let's not let this lesson fall through the cracks. Let's commit to do it!

Let's not be afraid! Pray through any fears or insecurities you might have? Be confident!

Don't worry you don't know enough. It is not hard to memorize the basic focus of each of the Steps of the Path2Strength and to remember what impacted you the most from each lesson. You can easily impart that much info to someone else and just refer back to your participation guide as needed.

They don't have to be long lessons. These small group sessions are designed to be long enough to achieve some level of spiritual growth *while* we are meeting together and to answer/work through most common objections or obstacles.

In an informal discipleship relationship, 10 – 15 minutes would probably be more than enough to teach someone the basics of the lesson and explain why it's important. Longer discussions would only be needed if there are objections or many questions.

Be structured. Not only should you follow-up with your disciple once per week to invite them into the next step, you should also be checking their progress on the last lesson. Don't forget to ask them to commit to whatever they need to commit to in order to fully embrace a lesson and put it into practice.

Let's go!

The Step of Joseph is about beginning to disciple others in order to obey the command of Our Lord & Savior, Jesus Christ.

Homework & Action Steps (5 min)

Action Steps

COMMIT to God in prayer your willingness to be a disciple-maker.

PRAY for Him to send you someone to disciple.

LOOK for 4 -5 people in your life who might need the Path2Strength.

ASK at least ONE of them what their relationship with God is like before we meet again.

Prayer (10-15 min)

Take a moment to pray for one another. Ask for any major prayer requests and ask certain members of the group to pray for others.

Repeat the requests slowly so everyone hears and those praying aren't embarrassed in the middle of their prayer by forgetting something.

(NOTE: 3 - 4 prayer requests is an ideal number. More than that can be overwhelming for the group to keep up with.)

STEP 12

MANASSEH - מנשה

"Forgetting"

THE WEAKNESS WE ARE STRENGTHENING

Many Christians are struggling with bitterness and hurt. They need to be free of this to move into full spiritual strength!

FOCUS

Forgiveness.

KEY VERSE

For if you forgive other people when they sin against you, your heavenly Father will also forgive you.
(Matthew 6:14)

KEY POINTS

- Forgiveness is a legal transaction, NOT an emotion or feeling.
- Name to God the people who hurt you and how they affected you.
- Then ask God to "not hold them accountable." This is dismissing the charges.
- Forgiving this way is the will of God for us.
- Forgiving does not mean forgetting. Remembering what took place so we won't repeat the same situation is wisdom.

The Step of Manasseh is about learning how to truly forgive.

The Study

Review (5 – 10 min)

REMIND about the **Step of Joseph**, i.e., beginning to disciple others!

1.) **ASK** *How did it go this week? Did anyone begin any spiritual conversations with anyone that could lead to intentional discipleship?*

Ice Breaker (20 min)

What is your biggest pet peeve in life?
(In a circle, everyone answers.)

Group Discussion (50 min)

Teaching

2.) **READ** the following passage to the group:

Then Peter came to Jesus and asked, "Lord, how many times shall I forgive my brother or sister who sins against me? Up to seven times?"

Jesus answered, "I tell you, not seven times, but seventy-seven times.

"Therefore, the kingdom of heaven is like a king who wanted to settle accounts with his servants. As he began the settlement, a man who owed him ten thousand bags of gold was brought to him. Since he was not able to pay, the master

ordered that he and his wife and his children and all that he had be sold to repay the debt.

"At this the servant fell on his knees before him. 'Be patient with me,' he begged, 'and I will pay back everything.' The servant's master took pity on him, canceled the debt and let him go.

"But when that servant went out, he found one of his fellow servants who owed him a hundred silver coins. He grabbed him and began to choke him. 'Pay back what you owe me!' he demanded.

"His fellow servant fell to his knees and begged him, 'Be patient with me, and I will pay it back.'

"But he refused. Instead, he went off and had the man thrown into prison until he could pay the debt. When the other servants saw what had happened, they were outraged and went and told their master everything that had happened.

"Then the master called the servant in. 'You wicked servant,' he said, 'I canceled all that debt of yours because you begged me to. Shouldn't you have had mercy on your fellow servant just as I had on you?' In anger his master handed him over to the jailers to be tortured, until he should pay back all he owed.

"This is how my heavenly Father will treat each of you unless you forgive your brother or sister from your heart."
(Matthew 18:21-35)

We often think of forgiveness as an emotional release of a grudge, but in the parable above, Jesus is equating a sin against someone with the creation of a legal debt.

Many Christians feel they have forgiven everyone in their life because they let things go easily, or they don't tend to hold grudges. But ignoring slights or releasing grudges are really just forms of extending grace. True forgiveness is a bigger thing. **It is to *legally* cancel a debt before a judge.**

Other Christians realize they have people in their life they should forgive, but can't bring themselves to do it because the injury is too large.

3.) ASK *Do you struggle with forgiveness? Is there anyone in particular you've struggled to forgive (that you're willing to share)?* (2-3 popcorn answers)

4.) ASK *Have you ever thought you forgave someone only to realize later you were still holding onto hurt and bitterness?* (2-3 popcorn answers)

Teaching

Many times, Christians think they have forgiven someone, but then they get surprised when that person's name comes up and they realize they still feel a tension, an uneasiness about their name. They don't want to think about the person at all. They believe they are not holding grudges, but they don't have a peace whenever that person is in their thoughts.

Joseph was the second-to-last son of Jacob (who was later renamed Israel by God.) His last son's name was Benjamin. Yet, we are not going to get to Benjamin for another two lessons.

The reason is that Jacob loved Joseph so much, at the end of his life, he blessed Joseph's two sons, Manasseh and Ephraim and raised them each up to full Tribe level, giving Joseph a double inheritance portion in Israel. (Genesis 48:8-21)

And it "happens" to be that the meanings of the names of the sons of Joseph correspond very well with two important steps on the Path2Strength!

The TWELFTH Step in the Path 2 Strength is the **STEP OF MANASSEH.**

The name Manasseh means "forgetting," and on the Path2Strength, we connect it with Forgiveness.

This may sound like an unusual lesson to include at this juncture, but Path2Hope has observed that a deeper understanding and practice of forgiveness is necessary for a believer to move into Strength, and we believe this is actually the perfect place for it in the order of the steps.

All Christians know forgiveness is a big part of Christianity. Of course, the focus is usually much more on our personal forgiveness through the Blood of Christ, and less on forgiving others.

Nevertheless, most Christians understand forgiving others was very important to Jesus, and they make an effort to do it. After all, Jesus said:

> *For if you forgive other people when they sin against you, your heavenly Father will also forgive you.*
> (Matthew 6:14)

Clearly, this is an important lesson. *Yet, most Christians think of forgiveness as an emotion.*

Let's repeat that: Most Christians think forgiveness is an emotion.

They try to let go of the feeling of being hurt or offended, they try to give grace. But then, when they remember past events and suddenly experience bouts of bitterness again, they beat themselves up, saying, "*What?* I thought I forgave them! I will have to forgive them again. Or maybe I will just have to keep forgiving them over and over again in my heart."

Others struggle to forgive because they aren't emotionally "ready" to forgive. The hurt is too great.

Both problems are because we are wrongly treating forgiveness like an emotion or a feeling.

> **Forgiveness is a legal transaction.**
> **It is to legally cancel a debt before a judge.**

Years ago, God took the Executive Director of Path2Hope, Zack Mason, on a very interesting journey of forgiveness.

Listen to his story:

I was headed to a weekend spiritual retreat as part of a ministry training program I was a part of. I was supposed to spend the weekend in a cabin, alone with God in prayer, and I wasn't even supposed to bring my own agenda to pray about. I was supposed to just listen for God and ask Him what He wanted to talk about.

Frankly, it was a pretty intimidating concept, but I agreed to do it. Right after I began the drive to the cabin, I told God, "Okay, I'm all yours."

*To my great shock, He **immediately** began speaking to me very clearly. And what He wanted to talk about was even more surprising.*

He began pressing me to call out loud to Him the name of every single person who had ever hurt me in order from my elementary school years to the present. And He not only wanted me to call out their names, He also wanted me to name the charges, meaning He wanted me to tell Him what they had done to me, as well as express to Him how it had made me feel.

It was like He was the judge, and I was pressing charges in His court.

*In that moment, he made me understand that **He had not forgotten any of these things.** He had not forgotten what these people had done to me, and He was not letting what they had done go, even if I had stopped thinking about it.*

This greatly surprised me. I think I had this impression, like I think most Christians feel, that God just wants us to go around letting stuff go and not be hurt by anything. Subconsciously, I'd been believing that He would say I was out of line if I treated any sins against me as being serious. I realized this had hurt my understanding of His love for me. Feeling like He just wanted me to let everything go all the time, subtly made me feel like He didn't care about me.

Realizing that He hadn't forgotten anything and that He intended to "prosecute" everyone who'd hurt me greatly magnified my appreciation of His love for me.

Nevertheless, I knew I had sinned against other people, and that He had canceled my debt through the payment of the Blood of Christ. Because I had benefitted in this way, I understood that He wanted me to extend the same benefit to others.

He wanted me to say to Him, "Father, please don't hold them accountable for what they did to me."

It was a legal transaction. He was asking if I was willing to "dismiss the charges" in a final way, never to be brought up again, so He wouldn't have to "prosecute" them.

I also understood that if I didn't say that to Him, then He was absolutely going to hold them accountable for whatever they'd done. Without me dismissing the charges in a formal way, He as the perfect judge, would execute judgment.

It meant if the person were not a follower in Christ, then what they had done to me was going to be part of what sent them to hell.

And if they were a Christian, then because their sins had all been paid for by the work of Christ on the Cross, then what they had done to me was going to be part of the sin burden Jesus carried on the cross.

Understanding this, I knew I didn't want to be part of the reason someone went to hell. I figured if someone went to hell for whatever else they had done to God or other people, so be it, but don't let them go to hell because of me.

And I DEFINITELY did not want to add to the sin burden on Jesus on the cross in any way. I felt like if I would ask God to "dismiss the charges" through formal forgiveness, then in a very tiny way, I could lift a little bit of the sin burden off of Jesus. **I definitely wanted to do that.**

So, as I did this, running through one name after the other, every time I said to God, "Father, please don't hold so-and-so accountable for what they did to me," I literally felt a physical knot release in my back!

The crazy thing is, I thought I had forgiven all of these people already. I had already made a big effort to forgive people emotionally. But God showed me that I was still holding onto those things as "offenses" even if I thought I'd forgiven them.

The only way to truly forgive someone and fully release it was to formally and legally ask the Judge to dismiss the charges. This is very different from just trying to "not feel angry or hurt anymore."

It took me almost two hours to go through everyone, and the process was unexpectedly exhausting. When I finally got to the cabin, I was so tired I crashed and slept for three hours.

I have repeated this process several times since then whenever I am hurt again by others. Every time, I have found that this process brings me great peace.

For example, a few years ago, a group of three people betrayed me in a very hurtful and lasting way. Since then, whenever I thought of their names, I would immediately begin to feel uneasy, tense, and upset.

Then, God reminded me of what I needed to do. He said, "Zack, isn't it time you did the process with them?" I said, "Yes, okay I guess." (Thinking maybe I wasn't ready but was willing to try.)

I did, and the next day, when I thought about their names, for this first time, I no longer felt tense or uneasy. Their names meant nothing to me anymore and I had a tremendous sense of peace.

I cannot recommend enough that every believer learn to treat forgiveness as a legal transaction between them and God like this. The benefits are enormous and wonderful.

5.) **ASK** *Does the story change your understanding of forgiveness? If so, how?* (2-3 popcorn answers)

Teaching

The exercise Zack described is very powerful. Rather than try to "feel" forgiveness for someone while you're hurt, it allows the believer to directly communicate with God and allow Him to do His job as judge.

Calling out to God the name of someone who has hurt you and telling Him what they did to you is like declaring the charges to the Judge. Explaining how it made you feel is bearing witness to the Judge of the impact of these offenses on you.

Asking Him to "not hold them accountable" is essentially asking the Judge to dismiss the charges. Only you have the legal authority to do that. Otherwise, the Judge will hold them accountable, either by having them pay the penalty personally, or by Jesus paying it for them.

God would not be the perfect judge if He just canceled everyone's debts against you without your permission. If you don't cancel the debt, the debt remains. It must be paid by that person, or by Jesus Himself if He has agreed to pay their debts for them,

NOTE: This does not mean a person could somehow escape the need to be saved through the Blood of Christ. Even if you and everyone else theoretically forgave a person their sins, everyone has also sinned against God Himself, and He requires the Blood of Christ as payment for those debts.

Jesus teaches us is that if we wish to be shown mercy, we must show mercy to others.

Here are some important points to remember:

Forgiveness is a legal transaction. We must ask God to dismiss the charges.

Dropping the charges against someone, doesn't mean forgetting. If you let someone borrow your car and they steal it, you don't let them borrow it again even if you've forgiven them. That is just wisdom.

Don't attempt this Forgiveness Exercise with your biggest hurts first. Start with smaller injuries, people that didn't hurt you that badly. Those will be easier and as you experience healing and freedom from those, it will encourage you to keep going and trust God with the larger ones.

Much healing should follow.

The Step of Manasseh is about learning to truly forgive.

Homework & Action Steps (5 min)

Action Steps

BEGIN talking to God this week about the people who have hurt you. Try to do the Forgiveness Exercise with at least 7 people from your past.

Prayer (10-15 min)

Take a moment to pray for one another. Ask for any major prayer requests and ask certain members of the group to pray for others.

Repeat the requests slowly so everyone hears and those praying aren't embarrassed in the middle of their prayer by forgetting something.

(NOTE: 3 - 4 prayer requests is an ideal number. More than that can be overwhelming for the group to keep up with.)

STEP 13

EPHRAIM - אפרים

"Doubly Fruitful"

LEADER'S NOTES

Spiritual warfare is real.

Spiritual warfare is on the increase.

We are all aware of the general downward path much of the world seems to be on. As long as this continues, it means we should logically expect that spiritual warfare will only increase as well.

In teaching believers about spiritual strength, we are remiss if we don't give them guidance about spiritual warfare.

What exactly is spiritual warfare? Paul explains to us in Ephesians 6:12:

> *For we do not wrestle against flesh and blood, but against principalities, against powers, against the rulers of the darkness of this age, against spiritual hosts of wickedness in the heavenly places.*

Both Christian and Jewish theologians say the terms "powers" and "principalities" as well as "rulers" are technical terms for certain ranks of angels that have been given different realms of authority in the physical world by God.

Some ranks of angels are in charge of managing the flow of history, others provide inspiration of ideas. Certain ranks of angels are in charge of political power and rule the affairs of cities, provinces, states, and even entire countries. For example, Daniel 10:13-14 teaches us that the angel that rules the country of Iran (which in the text is called the Prince of Persia) is a fallen angel. Michael the archangel is over God's people and fights angels like the Prince of Persia on our behalf.

Perhaps that may all sound like science fiction, but it is biblical. According to Revelation 12, when Satan fell, he took 1/3 of the angels with him. It would appear that many of the ones he took were the ones governing the political and cultural affairs of mankind.

This explains why the world systems always seem to be fighting against the Will of God.

Scripture also teaches us that when people **disobey** God's will, it somehow empowers the enemy's forces and allows them to more easily attack or influence us or others.

On the other hand, Scripture teaches that the prayers of a **righteous** person somehow add fuel to the armies of God and effect greater protection for ourselves and others.

This lesson will address the various aspect of spiritual warfare, including how the enemy tends to attack us, what we can do to fight it, etc.

Yet, in the face of what seems to be a clear increase in spiritual warfare in our country, Path2Hope is strongly recommending all believers adopt a prayer practice pastors have been using for many years effectively:

Establishing a personal prayer team.

The THIRTEENTH Step in the Path 2 Strength is the **STEP OF EPHRAIM.**

The name Ephraim means "Doubly Fruitful." The practice of establishing a personal prayer team for oneself has the very practical impact of doubling or even tripling the power of our prayers, as well as doubling the protection from spiritual attack we personally experience as others are praying for us more regularly.

This is based on what Jesus taught us:

> *For where two or three are gathered together in My name, I am there in the midst of them."*
> (Matthew 18:20)

Jesus gave us many tips on how to pray and how to make our prayers more effective. Here are some of the things God says can make a believer's prayer more powerful:

- Increased personal obedience
- Being in alignment with God's will ("in the name of Jesus")
- FAITH
- Persistence
- Fasting
- Being united in prayer with other Christians

Therefore, if a believer has a team of people who are joining him or her in prayer, persistently, and all are seeking to obey God more and more faithfully, and they even occasionally fast together, **won't their prayers be especially powerful?**

It is the experience of Path2Hope that believers who follow our recommendation to secure a team of seven personal prayer partners immediately experience significantly less spiritual warfare and feel their prayers answered much more quickly and frequently.

The Weakness We Are Strengthening

Many Christians are vulnerable to spiritual attack due to ongoing unrepentant sin. Yet, spiritual warfare has grown so strong that even faithful believers can find themselves under serious assault unless others are praying for them too.

Focus

Establishing a Personal Prayer Team

Key Verse

For where two or three are gathered together in My name, I am there in the midst of them."
(Matthew 18:20)

Key Points

- Spiritual warfare is REAL and on the increase.
- Disobedience to God empowers the enemy's forces.
- A righteous person's prayers add fuel to the armies of God.
- Obedience, faith, persistence, and fasting can make a believer's prayer more powerful, but we can be even more effective if we pray in numbers.
- Develop a prayer team – Invite other Christians to join you and pray for each other on a daily basis.

The Step of Ephraim is about establishing a personal prayer team.

THE STUDY

Review (5 – 10 min)

REMIND about the **STEP OF MANASSEH**, i.e., forgiveness.

Ice Breaker (20 min)

How did it go this last week with the homework? Did anyone have a breakthrough regarding forgiveness after doing the exercise?

(Up to 4 – 5 people can answer, popcorn style. Don't require everyone to answer. If no one answers, coach everyone and encourage them once again to do the forgiveness exercise this week.)

Group Discussion (50 min)

Teaching

This step on the Path2Strength is about understanding spiritual warfare and beginning to understand how to fight against it and be protected from it.

1.) ASK *Have you ever had a time when many things in your life were going wrong at the same time? Did you then consider you might be under spiritual attack? Why did you feel that way?* (2-3 popcorn answers)

Teaching

First, we need to understand what exactly spiritual warfare is. It's obviously a mystery in many ways to all of us, as none of us can see into the spiritual realm and understand what is happening.

Yet, the Bible gives us some hints, some insight into what is going on. Let's read together a few of those passages:

2.) READ: Ask group members to read the following verses:

Job 1:6-7 – *"Now there was a day when the sons of God [angels] came to present themselves before the Lord, and Satan also came among them. And the Lord said to Satan, "From where do you come?" So Satan answered the Lord and said, "From going to and fro on the earth, and from walking back and forth on it."*

Revelation 12:7-9 – *"And war broke out in heaven: Michael and his angels fought with the dragon; and the dragon and his angels fought, but they did not prevail, nor was a place found for them in heaven any longer. So, the great dragon was cast out, that serpent of old, called the Devil and Satan, who deceives the whole world; he was cast to the earth, and his angels were cast out with him.."*

[NOTE: The war in Heaven is ongoing right now. Revelation 12 is describing a future moment when the enemy and his angels will be defeated and thrown down to earth. None of them are cast into hell until after the 2nd Coming of Jesus.]

Daniel 10:2-14 – *"In those days I, Daniel, was mourning three full weeks. I ate no pleasant food, no meat or wine came into my mouth, nor did I anoint myself at all, till three whole weeks were fulfilled.*

Now on the twenty-fourth day of the first month, as I was by the side of the great river, that is, the Tigris, I lifted my eyes and looked, and behold, a certain man clothed in linen, whose waist was girded with gold of Uphaz! His body was like beryl, his face like the appearance of lightning, his eyes like torches of fire, his arms and feet like burnished bronze in color, and the sound of his words like the voice of a multitude.

And I, Daniel, alone saw the vision, for the men who were with me did not see the vision; but a great terror fell upon them, so that they fled to hide themselves. Therefore I was left alone when I saw this great vision, and no strength remained in me; for my vigor was turned to frailty in me, and I retained no strength. Yet, I heard the sound of his words; and while I heard the sound of his words I was in a deep sleep on my face, with my face to the ground.

Suddenly, a hand touched me, which made me tremble on my knees and on the palms of my hands. And he said to me, "O Daniel, man greatly beloved, understand the words that I speak to you, and stand upright, for I have now been sent to you." While he was speaking this word to me, I stood trembling.

Then he said to me, "Do not fear, Daniel, for from the first day that you set your heart to understand, and to humble yourself before your God, your words were heard; and I have come because of your words. But the prince of the kingdom of Persia withstood me twenty-one days; and behold, Michael, one of the chief princes, came to help me, for I had been left alone there with the kings of Persia. Now I have come to make you understand what will happen to your people in the latter days, for the vision refers to many days yet to come."

[NOTE: Many scholars believe that the "glorious man" in this vision speaking with Daniel was Jesus Himself. The Prince of Persia is a fallen angel who rules the country of Iran/Persia. Michael, the Archangel, is the governing angel over God's people. This passage indicates that Jesus Himself was held up for three weeks while Michael fought back the Prince of Persia.]

Ephesians 6:12 – *"For we do not wrestle against flesh and blood, but against **principalities**, against **powers**, against the **rulers** of the darkness of this age, against **spiritual hosts** of wickedness in the heavenly places."*

{NOTE: The terms "principalities," "powers," and "rulers" are technical terms for different ranks of angels.]

Exodus 17:8-13 – *"Now Amalek came and fought with Israel in Rephidim. And Moses said to Joshua, "Choose us some men and go out, fight with Amalek. Tomorrow I will stand on the top of the hill with the rod of God in my hand." So Joshua did as Moses said to him, and fought with Amalek. And Moses, Aaron, and Hur went up to the top of the hill. And so it was, when Moses held up his hand, that Israel prevailed; and when he let down his hand, Amalek prevailed. But Moses' hands became* heavy; so they took a stone and put it under him, and he sat on it. And Aaron and Hur supported his hands, one on one side, and the other on the other side; and his hands were steady until the going down of the sun. So Joshua defeated Amalek and his people with the edge of the sword."

Teaching

So, from these passages we understand that there is a war in Heaven that has been going on since the time of Adam & Eve. The devil in his pride convinced 1/3 of all the angels to rebel against God with him.

Hell was originally prepared for the devil and his angels as their punishment for this rebellion. The reason for the war in heaven is because the devil and his fallen angels want to take as many people with them there as they can. They want to do this for their own sick pleasure, because they know God loves people, and this is the only way they can hurt Him, by hurting God's heart.

This war is not happening right outside God's throne room. It is happening in another part of Heaven, some place in the spiritual realm that impacts events on earth.

Why did God allow this? Why does He allow this to go on when He could end it with a simple thought or Word? No man or woman can answer that question. Only God knows His own mind and *why* He feels it has to be this way. We just know it *is* this way.

Nevertheless, Ephesians and Exodus teach us that everything that happens on earth, good or bad, is simply a reflection of that war in Heaven.

Therefore, it is imperative that we learn to fight like Moses did. We must understand this spiritual reality and learn how to fight so we don't become victims of it.

The THIRTEENTH Step in the Path 2 Strength is the **STEP OF EPHRAIM.**

The name Ephraim means "Doubly Fruitful," and this step is about learning how to be protected from spiritual attack and make our prayers "doubly" effective.

3.) ASK *What are the most common ways the enemy attacks us?* (2-3 popcorn answers)

Teaching

The most common ways the enemy attacks us are:

- Temptations: lust, greed, gluttony, addictions, etc.
- Fear & Worry
- Inspiration to Anger
- Inspiration to Self-Righteousness
- Marriage problems
- Parenting problems
- Money problems

Typically, the enemy's forces will cycle through these problems with you trying to beat you down and separate you from God. They may inspire some problems between you and your spouse, but as soon as you work through those, some problems will arise with your children. Or maybe you are experiencing some problems with relationships at work, but as soon as those are resolved, we suddenly have money problems.

In general, we don't attribute these daily kinds of problems to spiritual warfare when they're happening one at a time, but they are. Yet, when the enemy gets strong and we are struggling in 2-3 of these areas all at the same time, we realize we are under spiritual attack.

The goal of Path2Hope is to help you move into a place of such spiritual strength that you are largely protected from most of these attacks and can experience a new peace.

We have some things to learn first.

4.) ASK *What are some ways you think of to make your prayers more effective? Why?* (2-3 popcorn answers)

Teaching

James 5:16-17 says:

> "Confess your trespasses to one another, and pray for one another, that you may be healed. **The effective, fervent prayer of a righteous man avails much.** Elijah was a man with a nature like ours, and he prayed earnestly that it would not rain; and it did not rain on the land for three years and six months. And he prayed again, and the heaven gave rain, and the earth produced its fruit."

What James is teaching us is that a Christian's level of obedience determines how effective their prayers are. The more obedient one of God's children is, the more He listens to them and gives them what they are asking.

Disobedience, then, opens us up to spiritual attack. Every time you fall back into habitual sin, you are empowering the enemy's forces in the war in Heaven.

Also, even if we are personally obedient, the more people around us in society are disobeying God, the more power the enemy's forces have against everyone corporately.

Nevertheless, pursuing righteousness, seeking to obey God as much as possible will increase the power of your prayers.

Along those same lines, Jesus said:

> And whatever you ask **in My name**, that I will do, that the Father may be glorified in the Son.
> (John 14:13)

That phrase "in my name" does not mean just to end a prayer "in the name of Jesus" as if it were some magical phrase. In the ancient world, to come to someone in someone else's name meant to be speaking as their messenger, or their ambassador.

Even today, we understand this. If a man in a suit came to your door and said, "I come to you in the name of the President of the United

States," you would understand the president had sent him with a message for you.

Therefore, Jesus is teaching us to pray to the Father as an ambassador of Himself, which means we are to pray in alignment with Jesus' will. If we do so, then we are also **in alignment with God's will, because there is no daylight between the will of the Son and the will of the Father**. Therefore, God will always answer those prayers. If we pray in faith for something Jesus wants, the Father will do it.

Also, Jesus made it clear that **FAITH** has a huge role in the effectiveness of our prayers:

So, Jesus answered and said to them, "Assuredly, I say to you, if you have faith and do not doubt, you will not only do what was done to the fig tree, but also if you say to this mountain, 'Be removed and be cast into the sea,' it will be done. And whatever things you ask in prayer, believing, you will receive."
(Matthew 21:21-22)

5.) READ: Ask a group member to read the following parable of Jesus:

Then He spoke a parable to them, that men always ought to pray and not lose heart, saying: "There was in a certain city a judge who did not fear God nor regard man. Now there was a widow in that city; and she came to him, saying, 'Get justice for me from my adversary.' And he would not for a while; but afterward he said within himself, 'Though I do not fear God nor regard man, yet because this widow troubles me I will avenge her, lest by her continual coming she weary me.' "

Then the Lord said, "Hear what the unjust judge said. And shall God not avenge His own elect who cry out day and night to Him, though He bears long with them? I tell you that He will avenge them speedily. Nevertheless, when the Son of Man comes, will He really find faith on the earth?"
(Luke 18:1-8)

Teaching

What Jesus is teaching us in that parable is that ***persistence*** increases the effectiveness of our prayers.

6.) READ: Ask a group member to read the following story about Jesus:

And when He came to the disciples, He saw a great multitude around them, and scribes disputing with them. Immediately, when they saw Him, all the people were greatly amazed, and running to Him, greeted Him. And He asked the scribes, "What are you discussing with them?"

Then one of the crowd answered and said, "Teacher, I brought You my son, who has a mute spirit. And wherever it seizes him, it throws him down; he foams at the mouth, gnashes his teeth, and becomes rigid. So I spoke to Your disciples, that they should cast it out, but they could not."

He answered him and said, "O faithless generation, how long shall I be with you? How long shall I bear with you? Bring him to Me." Then they brought him to Him. And when he saw Him, immediately the spirit convulsed him, and he fell on the ground and wallowed, foaming at the mouth.

So He asked his father, "How long has this been happening to him?"

And he said, "From childhood. And often he has thrown him both into the fire and into the water to destroy him. But if You can do anything, have compassion on us and help us."

Jesus said to him, "If you can believe, all things are possible to him who believes."

Immediately the father of the child cried out and said with tears, "Lord, I believe; help my unbelief!"

When Jesus saw that the people came running together, He rebuked the unclean spirit, saying to it, "Deaf and dumb spirit, I command you, come out of him and enter him no more!" Then the spirit cried out, convulsed him greatly, and came out of him. And he became as one dead, so that many said, "He is dead." But Jesus took him by the hand and lifted him up, and he arose.

And when He had come into the house, His disciples asked Him privately, "Why could we not cast it out?"

So He said to them, "This kind can come out by nothing but prayer and fasting."
(Mark 9:14-29)

Teaching

What Jesus is teaching us here is that ***fasting*** increases the effectiveness of our prayers.

Lastly, Jesus teaches us that the number of believers praying in unity for something has a greater impact as well:

7.) READ: Ask a group member to read the following words of Jesus:

Again, I say to you that if two of you agree on earth concerning anything that they ask, it will be done for them by My Father in heaven. For where two or three are gathered together in My name, I am there in the midst of them."
(Matthew 18:19-20)

Teaching

In summary, these are the things that make our prayers more effective:

- Increased personal obedience
- Being in alignment with God's will ("in the name of Jesus")
- FAITH

- Persistence
- Fasting
- Being united in prayer with other Christians

A Christian who pursues righteousness, is in tune with God's will, is persistent in their prayers, and BELIEVES God is listening to them and loves them and will look upon their request with favor will see a HUGE increase in answered prayer.

Such prayers are like fuel to the armies of God in the war in Heaven.

Fasting of course can strengthen our prayers as well.

However, in this age of severe degradation, in this time in history where society at large is turning its collective back on God, Path2Hope strongly recommends a specific prayer practice to protect yourself against the stronger levels of spiritual warfare that are being felt.

Path2Hope recommends working to establish a seven-person prayer team for yourself, one for every day of the week. Many pastors have done this for generations.

What does that mean? How does one go about it?

Think about other Christians you know who you think might be open to it and invite them to join you on a specific day each week.

In other words, ask a believer you trust to be your Monday prayer partner and someone else to be your Tuesday prayer partner, etc. This means you and that believer are agreeing to pray for each other that day.

It is not good practice to just message your entire group once per week with your current requests and asking them to send theirs. That is not effective.

On Monday, you and your Monday prayer partner should communicate, even if it's just briefly through text about each other's current prayer needs, and you've both agreed to pray for each other that day over those things. You do the same for each day of the week.

When inviting people to join you in this, you can ask if they would be willing to do it for one year, and every year you can check with each other if they are wanting to continue. This keeps people from feeling like they are obligating themselves to be your partner for the rest of their lives.

If you don't have seven people in mind you can approach, start with one or two. Get a personal prayer team started with just those and then you can pray for God to lead you to more prayer partners.

You should also encourage all of your prayer partners to get 7 prayer partners themselves!

Any believer who does this will not only experience a significant and noticeable increase in their spiritual protection and the effectiveness of their prayers, but they will feel a wonderfully deepened sense of community and closeness with these friends you're praying with.

How Do You Know If You Need A Personal Prayer Team?

Do you ever struggle with any of the following?

- **Depression**
- **Anxiety**
- **Fear**
- **Anger**
- **Apathy**
- **Lust**
- **Greed**
- **Pride**
- **Envy/Covetousness**

Those are standard thoughts/emotions that the enemy's forces throw at us. Once we grab onto any of these thoughts, they are empowered to provoke a cycle of negative thoughts in our minds and hearts. They do this to get strength against us and others, fueled by our sin.

When we are stuck in a cyclical attack like this, it can be difficult to escape without help.

A personal prayer team lifting you up regularly will almost always make a huge difference.

8.) ASK *What do you think about this idea of establishing a personal prayer team? Do you have people in mind you think you could approach this week?* (4-5 popcorn answers)

Teaching

One more very practical tip. If you need immediate relief from an assault of continual negative thoughts and emotions, begin praising God verbally out loud for who He is and what He has done around your home/space. You normally will feel a distinct lightening of the atmosphere.

Why does this work? The enemy's forces cannot stand to be in the presence of God being praised, so when you begin praising Him out loud, they have to leave for a time.

Still, this is no substitute for a personal prayer team which will have a much larger and longer impact!

The Step of Ephraim is about establishing a personal prayer team.

Homework & Action Steps (5 min)

Action Steps

COMMIT to inviting 2 – 3 people to be prayer partners with you, each for a different day of the week. Begin praying with them.

Prayer (10-15 min)

Take a moment to pray for one another. Ask for any major prayer requests and ask certain members of the group to pray for others.

Repeat the requests slowly so everyone hears and those praying aren't embarrassed in the middle of their prayer by forgetting something.

(NOTE: 3 - 4 prayer requests is an ideal number. More than that can be overwhelming for the group to keep up with.)

STEP 14

BENJAMIN - בִּנְיָמִין

"Son of the Right Hand"

LEADER'S NOTES

The FOURTEENTH Step in the Path 2 Strength is the **STEP OF BENJAMIN.**

(Note we did not say the LAST step because a believer should always be taking more steps toward spiritual strength, but this is the LAST step of this course.)

Be sure to review all the information under the "Group Discussion" section of this lesson so you're familiar with the meaning of the name Benjamin, its cultural significance, and the information about depression and ego.

Leader, please know that ALL of your group members are struggling with different ego issues (as are you.) We know this because they're human. All of us humans struggle with various ego issues.

Sometimes, ego is easy to see. Those who are arrogant or brag or show some other lack of humility are not hard to identify as having a pride issue, but there are other ways in which excessive ego/pride manifests itself (insecurity, depression, and fear). Again, be sure to review these before the lesson.

SPECIAL NOTE

Leader, thank you so much for leading your group through the Path2Strentgth course. It is our hope that you have been blessed with seeing the countenances of your group members change over the past few months. It is normal to see believers who begin with much fear and insecurity move into a place of clear strength.

We love seeing that!

It is also our hope that you will either continue to lead this small group going forward, or that you will have raised up co-leaders during this course who can take over leadership as you transition out.

Either way, we hope your group will continue meeting to study other things together AND that your group will continue to do at least one monthly neighborhood outreach going forward.

This is one of the primary goals of Path2Hope in creating the Path2Strength course. It is not only to help believers become strong, but to put more workers into the field to expand the Kingdom of God.

We humbly ask that you consider helping make this happen. Please read the conclusion of this booklet for more details.

THE WEAKNESS WE ARE STRENGTHENING

All of us Christians struggle with a variety of sins or negative traits that are ego based. Pursuing humility will not only allow us to overcome those, but it will truly allow us to uplift Jesus as King of Kings and Lord of Lords.

FOCUS

Pursuing humility.

KEY VERSE

He has shown you, O man, what is good;
And what does the Lord require of you but to do justly, to love
mercy, and to walk humbly with your God?
(Matthew 18:20)

Key Points

- Humble yourself before God.
- Lift Jesus up by decreasing yourself.
- ALL of us struggle with some type of ego issue because we are human.
- Embracing your true value in God will diminish negative ego issues.
- Pride cannot survive sincere gratitude.

The Study

Review (5 – 10 min)

REMIND about the **Step of Ephraim**, i.e., establishing a personal prayer team.

Ice Breaker (20 min)

How did it go this last week with the homework? How many prayer partners does everyone have now?

(Go in a circle. Let everyone talk about their progress. This gently reinforces the need to push forward with this project.)

Group Discussion (50 min)

Teaching

Welcome to the last lesson of the Path2Strength course! We've had some amazing conversations on this journey.

1.) ASK *We'd like to take a minute and share how this course has helped you and your walk with God. How has your relationship with God deepened? In what ways do you feel spiritually stronger.* (4 – 5 popcorn answers)

Teaching

At the end of this lesson, we're going to talk about how to keep this group going, how to not lose the progress we've made, and how to expand the movement to help other Christians grow strong!

But first we need to talk about the Step of Benjamin

The FOURTEENTH Step in the Path 2 Strength is the **STEP OF BENJAMIN.**

The name Benjamin means "Son of the Right Hand," and it is pointing to Jesus as King of Kings and Ruler of the Universe.

Cultural Note: In ancient times, the right hand was considered the "good hand" and the left hand was considered the "dirty hand." This was not an attack on left-handed people . . . it was simply before the existence of toilet paper. The right hand was used for everything clean, eating, shaking hands with people, etc., and the left hand was used for . . . well, for cleaning oneself and other dirty tasks. Therefore, whoever sat the king's right hand was the top official, whoever sat the left side of the king was the #3 official of the kingdom.

Jesus being called the "Son of the Right Hand" means He rules at the right hand of the God the Father.

The **STEP OF BENJAMIN** is about honoring Jesus as King and lifting Him up. This is done by humbling ourselves before Him.

The best and easiest way to lift someone up is to lower yourself. **To lift yourself up is to compete with them for "glory."**

Thus, when speaking about Jesus, John the Baptist said,

> *He must increase, but I must decrease.*
> (John 3:30)

So, this is what we must do as well. We must decrease so that Christ can increase.

This will benefit our relationship with God in many ways, for as we know He opposes the proud. Therefore, He is drawn to the humble.

James 4:6 says:

> *"God resists the proud but gives grace to the humble."*

The whole of Scripture teaches that humility is a condition for not only approaching God but staying close to Him.

This will also allow the Kingdom of God to expand faster among men because Jesus said that when He is lifted up, He will draw all men unto Himself.

So, this lesson is simply about pursuing humility. It's a very simple concept, but it's hard for us to do.

2.) ASK *What are some of the typical signs of a person struggling with pride?* (2 - 3 popcorn answers)

Teaching

It may surprise you to know that the following are *also* signs we may have a pride/ego problem and need to pursue greater humility:

- You feel certain tasks are beneath you.
- The topic of most conversations is "you" or what's going on in your life, rather than the other person.
- You say things like, "That's just how I am" when confronted with a flaw.
- Overly independent and relying on self
- An unteachable spirit.
- Defensiveness
- Never willing to apologize
- In need of constant praise, attention, or admiration
- Envious of others
- Overly obsessed with physical appearance
- Overly concerned with what others think.
- Oversensitive
- Entitled
- Ungrateful
- Self-righteousness
- Condescending

Teaching

Rather than think about friends or family (or even enemies) we know who struggle with these things, we should focus on whether or not we recognize any of these signs in ourselves.

3.) **ASK** *Did any of those signs surprise you? Which of those did you recognize in yourself?* (2 - 3 popcorn answers)

Teaching

Truly, when you think about it, since all sin is a form of selfishness and/or rebelliousness, **then all sin is rooted in an ego problem of some kind.**

If we want God's favor, we must pursue humility.

4.) **READ:** Ask group members to read the following verses:

Proverbs 11:2 – *"When pride comes, then comes shame; but with the humble is wisdom."*

Romans 12:16 – *"Live in harmony with one another. Do not be proud, but be willing to associate with people of low position. Do not be conceited." (NIV)*

1 Peter 3:3-4 – *"Do not let your adornment be merely outward — arranging the hair, wearing gold, or putting on fine apparel — rather let it be the hidden person of the heart, with the incorruptible beauty of a gentle and quiet spirit, which is very precious in the sight of God.*

James 4:10 – *"Humble yourselves in the sight of the Lord, and He will lift you up."*

Colossians 3:12 – *"Therefore, as the elect of God, holy and beloved, put on tender mercies, kindness, humility, meekness, longsuffering."*

Proverbs 29:23 – *"A man's pride will bring him low, but the humble in spirit will retain honor."*

Proverbs 22:4 – *"Humility is the fear of the Lord; its wages are riches and honor and life." (NIV)*

1 Peter 5:6 – *"Humble yourselves, therefore, under God's mighty hand, that he may lift you up in due time." (NIV)*

2 Chronicles 7:14 – *"If My people who are called by My name will humble themselves, and pray and seek My face, and turn from their wicked ways, then I will hear from heaven, and will forgive their sin and heal their land."*

Teaching

When people are arrogant, or bragging and boastful, it's easy to see their pride. Yet, here are some unexpected ways ego problems can be seen in our lives:

A.) **Severe insecurity**. A person who overly berates themselves, or feels they have no real significance to the Kingdom of God has an ego problem, albeit a negative version of it and opposite that of the boastful person.

A believer who feels this level of worthlessness is not recognizing how valuable they are in God's eyes and the gifts He has put into them. **This is an ego problem because they are valuing their own opinion of themselves more than God's words about them.**

Boastful people have an overinflated view of their value and importance; insecure people underestimate their value and importance. Both are defining themselves with their own thoughts rather than God's.

B.) **Depression** is also often an ego issue. (*NOTE: we don't mean "feeling wounded" or "hurt", we mean depression.*) When we are depressed, our minds experience an unceasing whirlwind of negative thoughts *about ourselves*.

This is a self-centered state, though it's a negative form of self-centeredness. The best solution to depression is usually to get out of our own heads, to stop thinking about ourselves *at all*, and begin focusing on loving others.

IMPORTANT NOTE: Severe clinical depression and/or suicidal thoughts are serious and can be caused by a chemical imbalance which is a physical imbalance. *We are not talking about that level of depression, or severe spiritual trauma. In such cases, a believer should immediately seek the help of a qualified pastor or licensed counselor.*

C.) **Fear** is also an issue of ego. Fear and anxiety are rooted in a conscious or subconscious belief that the only one we can trust is ourselves.

When we successfully learn to not lean on ourselves, but to trust in God for our needs and protection, fear and anxiety fall away.

Therefore, as we learn to lift Jesus up by decreasing ourselves, we not only become spiritually more attractive, but things like fear, anger, and depression dissipate.

5.) **ASK** *Does it surprise you that negative emotions like insecurity, depressions, and fear can be rooted in ego?* (2 - 3 popcorn answers)

Teaching

So, how do we overcome these ego issues? *How do we pursue humility while retaining joy?*

There are two practices you can do regularly to keep yourself on the right track with humility:

Embrace Your True Value

Accepting your true value in God is an identity issue and it will solve the negative ego issues like anxiety, fear, depression, and insecurity.

You are a son or daughter of God. He took a lot of time to weave you together in your mother's womb and He loves you dearly. You are of immense value to Him. Jesus would have still chosen to die on the cross even if it was just for you.

Practice **disbelieving** all the negativity that has been spoken into you over the years and instead **embrace in faith** all that God has promised and said about you and your value. Practice this daily. Remind yourself of it.

Don't just believe it in your head, let the truth of your value sink into your heart.

To not believe that you are valuable to Him, is to *disbelieve God*, which is a sin. To accept His words about your value, is to *believe Him*. It is **Faith, which the Bible says is credited to us as righteousness.**

Gratitude

This one is pretty simple. Expressing gratitude to God as a daily practice during our prayer time will keep you off the path of arrogance, boasting, and self-righteousness.

The more grateful to Him you are, the more humble before Him you will be. Practice **expressing** gratitude to Him for everything from the country you were born in, the talents and gifts you have, your daily food and provision, and even every time you have successfully obeyed Him.

Pride cannot survive sincere gratitude.

The Step of Benjamin is about pursuing humility to lift Jesus up.

Prayer (10-15 min)

Take a moment to pray for one another. Ask for any major prayer requests and ask certain members of the group to pray for others.

Repeat the requests slowly so everyone hears and those praying aren't embarrassed in the middle of their prayer by forgetting something.

Conclusion (5 – 10 min)

You have now finished the Path2Strength course!

It is our hope at Path2Hope that you not only feel significantly stronger after completing this course, but that you will invite others into it and help keep the movement going.

We would like you to consider doing the following:

1.) **Continue to meet as a group.** Many of you have probably grown close over the last 14 weeks. Let's not let that sense of community go! Choose a book of the Bible or another study topic and keep going!

2.) **Commit to keep doing outreach.** There are too many broken people in the world. We can't reach them all with the Gospel without you!

    Path2Hope has launched these groups not only to strengthen believers, but also to expand greatly the amount of outreach happening. Let's build the Kingdom together!

    It's up to your group to choose how many times per month (we usually recommend 1 – 2 times per month) and what day and time you go out.

3.) **Disciple others.** Be intentional about teaching others the steps of the Path2Strength. You will love seeing them grow stronger and feel more joy as they walk with you.

4.) Invite other small group leaders to consider taking their group members through the Path2Strength.

We at Path2Hope are very grateful for you and pray that His favor and grace and peace will be upon you always.

APPENDIX A

THE GOLDEN ALTAR OF INCENSE
(*What & When* to Pray)

This golden altar inside the Temple was much smaller than the bronze one outside. The golden altar was used for burning incense and *only for burning incense.*

There is absolutely no doubt about the symbolic meaning of incense. We know from Scripture that the earthly Temple was simply a replica of a greater Temple that actually exists in Heaven. Revelation 8:3-4 makes it very clear what the incense on the golden altar represents:

Another angel, who had a golden censer, came and stood at the altar. He was given much incense to offer, with the prayers of all God's people, on the golden altar in front of the throne. The smoke of the incense, together with the prayers of God's people, went up before God from the angel's hand. (Revelation 8:3-4, NIV)

Just as the Golden Altar of Incense stood before the Ark of the Covenant in Solomon's Temple, so does the heavenly Golden Altar stand before God's throne in Heaven. Apparently, your and my prayers are offered before God in Heaven as if it were incense on the altar.

Again, we see the same comparison in Revelation 5:8:

And when he had taken it, the four living creatures and the twenty-four elders fell down before the Lamb. Each one had a harp and they were holding golden bowls full of incense, which are the prayers of God's people. (NIV)

God is telling us that prayer is one of the three ways we are to

seek Him.

So, a logical follow-up question you may have is *how* then should we pray? Meaning what words should we use?

We all know we should pray.

The Bible says we should pray.

It's nice to know that God is focusing us on prayer as one of the three main spiritual habits we should pursue, but *what* does he want the nature of our prayers to be?

I believe God has given us that answer as well.

He's given us the answer *symbolically* in the description of the incense that He commanded to be offered, and He gave it to us again in the New Testament when the disciples asked Jesus, "Lord, how should we pray?"

The Temple Incense

Why should you care about something as obscure as the Temple Incense?

Because God does.

See what He said to Moses about it:

Then the Lord said to Moses, "Take for yourself spices, stacte *and* onycha *and* galbanum, *spices with* pure frankincense; *there shall be an equal part of each. With it you shall make incense, a perfume, the work of a perfumer, salted, pure, and holy. You shall beat some of it very fine, and put part of it before the testimony in the tent of meeting where I will meet with you; it shall be most holy to you. The incense which you shall make, you shall not make in the same proportions for yourselves; it shall be holy to you for the Lord. Whoever shall make any like it, to use as perfume, shall be cut off from his people." (Exodus 30:34-38)*

In other words, God gave Moses a *very* specific formula to make this incense *and* He told him that if anyone tried to make the same formula for their own home *that they were to be killed*.

The death penalty for re-creating an incense formula.

That should tell us that there is something important to understand about this formula. If God considered it that important, then we should also consider it important and ask ourselves *why* it's important. We should seek to understand it.

Since incense is a confirmed symbol for prayer, God is giving us a very large hint that He is laying out His preferred formula for prayer — a *holy* formula for prayer.

Of course, any spiritual truth about prayer we might glean would have to be interpreted symbolically from the various elements.

Scholars, Rabbis, and Christian theologians are all in universal agreement that the most important elements of the incense are the four ingredients God gives us by name.

They are: *stacte*, *onycha*, *galbanum*, and *frankincense*.

Most reputable scholars have identified the first two as Styrax benzoin (gum resin) and Labdanum respectively, both of which drip from their source trees like tear drops. Galbanum is still known by that name today and is distinct from the other ingredients in that it has a very pungent, bitter smell. (The others are all sweet-smelling.)

The origin of the name Frankincense means "incense of the highest quality." The more ancient name was Olibanum, and while it also bleeds from its tree like tear drops, it has a very light, sweet scent.

Let's take a step back for a second and examine what Jesus' answered His disciples when they asked Him how *they* should pray.

He taught them the most famous of all prayers: the Lord's Prayer.

Curiously (really it's not so curious), the Lord's Prayer seems to have four distinct parts that can easily be seen to correspond with the four ingredients of the Temple Incense.

Stacte

He said, *Pray, then, in this way:*

'Our Father who is in Heaven, hallowed be Your Name. Your Kingdom come. Your will be done, on earth as it is in Heaven . . .'

If you're like me, you may have tended to rush through these first verses of the Lord's Prayer in the past, eager to get to the "give us this day our daily bread" part. I know I've always tended to view the first lines as a "majestic" part of the prayer, focused on giving God glory.

But what if we've been reading those first lines with the wrong tone?

What if instead of a confident declaration this is actually a crying out? What if the tone is *Oh my father, how long until you redeem the earth. There is so much injustice, so much brokenness, my dear Father in Heaven, how long until Your will is done on earth as it is in Heaven?*

Stacte, the first ingredient of the Holy Incense, means "drops," as in teardrops. The original Hebrew word is *nataf*, which means the same thing. This alludes to crying out in prayer. I believe the first part of the Lord's Prayer is actually a crying out over *the state of the world*, and that is represented in the Old Testament by *stacte*.

In modern day, we refer to *nataf/stacte* as Benzoin.

Benzoin has some very interesting properties that correlate it strongly with the first section of the Lord's Prayer.

First, Benzoin drops are gathered by wounding a mature Styrax Benzoin tree.

In the same way, if we cry out to God over the state of the world, longing for its redemption, isn't it because we ourselves have been wounded by it? Even as we cry out for others, aren't we ourselves hurt by their pain?

When burned as incense, Benzoin emits a sweet, warm, and

***vanilla*-like aroma.**

If someone tells you that vanilla is their favorite ice cream flavor, don't you look at them twice? The reason is because vanilla is a very simple, *generic* scent/taste. We expect more complex combinations to be someone's favorite, like mint chocolate chip or Rocky Road.

The vanilla scent of Benzoin speaks to the generalized nature of our prayers over the state of the world. Such prayers are not complex or personalized because we don't know as much about other people or their situations as we do ourselves. These prayers are simpler because they are so large in scope.

Benzoin oil is golden-brown in color, which points to the divine-earthly (golden-brown) connection.

May Your Will in Heaven (gold) be done on earth (brown). May Your golden Will be brought down to the brown soil of our habitation.

Importantly, in the art of perfumery, benzoin is commonly used as a *fixative*, meaning it is a substance that retains the power of other aromas longer, keeping them from dispersing rapidly into the air.

In the same way, when I begin a prayer pleading for the world or even just my community at large, it tends to have a focusing effect on the rest of my prayer. It centers me on the things that concern God, rather than losing focus on distractions that shouldn't be important to me but are.

A Kingdom-focused prayer can be a *fixative* for the rest of your prayers.

Lastly, Benzoin has a *lot* of medicinal uses.

Every one of them involves the reduction of harmful bacteria and/or relieving stress.

Kingdom-oriented prayers have the same effect on us. When I regularly spend time praying for those trapped in sex trafficking, I am much less likely to fall prey to spiritual bacteria like the name-it-and-claim-it, wealth-oriented theologies. I also tend to find my stress levels reduced as I remember that my little world isn't that big after all, and that God is sovereign and in control.

Onycha

"Give us this day our daily bread . . ."

The second ingredient in the Temple Incense is *onycha*.

Onycha is a Greek word meaning "fingernail" or "claw" and the best scholarship identifies this as labdanum, a substance that is derived from the rockrose bush. The flowers of the rockrose bush have petals with scarlet fingernail-shaped markings. These markings turn black as they mature.

Raw labdanum resin is usually dark-amber-green but turns black later. It is somewhat malleable at first then becomes brittle as it ages.

The Hebrew name for this essence is *shecheleth* and means "roaring (like a lion)." It has this name because labdanum was originally cultivated by Egyptians who harvested it by combing drops of the resin out of goats' beards. The temperamental animals would roar from pain as the sticky drops were removed from their hair.

Simultaneously, the Hebrew word *shecheleth* is also related to the Syriac *shehelta* which is translated as "a tear" and the Aramaic *shchl*, which signifies "to retrieve."

Onycha, like *stacte*, represents a crying out to God. in our prayer, but for our personal petitions rather than kingdom-wide prayers. It corresponds to the second part of the Lord's Prayer, *"Give us this day our daily bread."*

Like *stacte*, the Hebrew word for *onycha* also relates to "teardrop," referring to our pain as we rarely ask God for help with things that aren't hurting or frustrating us. We roar at God like the goats of old as this part of the essence of our prayer is only cultivated in our pain.

Of course, the last linguistic connection is "to retrieve" which clearly reflects what we are trying to accomplish by asking God for our daily bread.

Like *stacte*, *onycha* (or labdanum) has an amber-like scent.
(Vanilla is considered part of the amber fragrance family.) That fact together with the teardrop association clearly indicates that both *stacte* and *onycha* represent types of prayer that are similar in substance: a crying out of a man or woman of God in need.

Yet, *onycha* comes from a bush rather than a tree like *stacte*. This is because *stacte* represents larger, broader, kingdom-oriented prayers and *onycha* represents the smaller, more personal petitions.

Like *stacte*, *onycha* is also used as a fixative in the perfume industry, which means that our personal petitions also help keep the rest of our prayers focused on the right things.

Labdanum (*onycha*) resin is primarily produced by boiling the leaves and twigs of the rockrose bush.
The leaves and twigs represent that which is pruned from a believer by the Master Cultivator and then subjected to the Refiner's fire (the boiling.)

God's uses the trials and frustrations of our lives to produce growth in us, and He wants us to bring Him our needs and wants in prayer. *That* is confirmed by His mandatory inclusion of *onycha* in the formula for the Temple Incense.

One last thought here: Labdanum resin becomes brittle and black with age.
Therefore, if we fail to bring our petitions to God in a timely manner, our hearts can also become blackened and bitter.
So, bring Him the Onycha prayer freshly.

Galbanum

"... And forgive us our debts, as we also have forgiven our debtors.
And do not lead us into temptation, but deliver us from evil ..."

Galbanum is very different from the other ingredients in that it is the only one of the four that has a bitter scent rather than a sweet one.

Rashi, one of history's most celebrated Jewish rabbis and a well-respected commentator on the first books of the Bible, said that galbanum was included in the Temple Incense to remind us of deliberate and unrepentant sinners.

Galbanum initially gives off a very bitter and peculiar smell, followed by an intense "green" aroma. In perfumery, the green family of fragrances includes everything from green apples to evergreen trees. Specifically, galbanum has been described as a very complex, woodsy smell as if you'd broken open a fresh stalk or pod of peas.

From personal experience, I can tell you that when galbanum is burned, the smell is actually sickening. I tested it and found myself wanting to blow out the flame very quickly after heating it.

This third ingredient corresponds exactly to the third part of the Lord's Prayer, confession of sins.

The bitter portion of the scent represents the poisonous nature of our sins within us. Bitterness is a symbol for poison. The Bible often uses plants and trees as symbols for people, especially believers, so the "green" aspect of the smell represents the life within us being bled out by these sins.

Galbanum gum resin is yellow-green or yellow-brown and looks exactly like vomit. You can't help but be reminded of Revelation 3:16 where Jesus says he will vomit those lukewarm, sinful believers out of his mouth.

If those identifiers weren't enough, galbanum resin contains significant amounts of sulfur . . . which always symbolizes sin.

God included galbanum in the Temple Incense to remind us that confession is a necessary part of our prayers. This also ties back to the purpose of the Bronze Sea outside the Temple. If we don't allow God to regularly cleanse our hands and feet of the dirt we've picked up traveling through the world, He will have no part with us.

I would disagree with Rashi in one aspect. He said that galbanum was included to remind us of the unrepentant sinners around us. I would say that God included galbanum to remind us of the unrepentant sinner *within* us.

Frankincense

"For Yours is the Kingdom and the power and the glory forever. Amen."

Frankincense is well-known. It was one of the three gifts the magi brought to Jesus at His birth. Its name literally means "incense of the highest quality."

It has a light, lemony scent with a pine-like undertone. This fourth ingredient of the Temple Incense corresponds to the fourth and final section of the Lord's prayer: Praise!

In prayer, we praise God for who He is and for what He has done.

Examining its characteristics, Frankincense helps us to understand this even better.

Frankincense trees can grow in unforgiving places.

The official name of Frankincense is *Olibanum* and it is cultivated from the *Boswellia* tree. Specifically, the *Boswellia Sacra* (Sacred Boswellia tree) which has a very unusual feature. The Sacred Boswellia can grow in very hostile environments, so much so they can even grow out of solid rock. The way in which they grow out of the rock is so secure that even violent storms are unable to rip them out.

Of course, this is reminiscent of you and I as believers being rooted in the solid rock foundation which is Jesus Christ. If we are rooted in Him, we cannot be uprooted.

"And the rain descended, the floods came, and the winds blew and beat on that house; and it did not fall, for it was founded on the rock." (Matthew 7:25)

Sacred Boswellia trees are often described as scraggly, but hardy trees.

> *"For He shall grow up before Him as a tender plant,*
> *and as a root out of dry ground.*
> *He has no form or comeliness; and when we see Him,*
> *there is no beauty that we should desire Him."*
> (Isaiah 53:2)

It is known that Jesus was not especially attractive in a physical way. God chose to not gift Him with a special handsomeness in order to bring greater glory to His name.

No one can claim that people were attracted to the ministry of Jesus simply because He was handsome or charismatic.

On the contrary, Jesus is the founder of the greatest movement the world has ever seen, yet it happened solely because of who He is and the power of God within Him.

So, He was "scraggly" in form, yet His essence is very hardy. He was not a *"reed shaken by the wind."* Our Messiah endured more than anyone, and in every way.

Frankincense smells fresh.

The light, lemony freshness of the aroma of Frankincense stands for the fresh new life we have in Christ Jesus. Nothing smells cleaner than lemons, and so we sense through the aroma that Christ has also cleansed us of our sins.

Frankincense is cultivated by striping the trees.

> *"And by His stripes we are healed."*
> *(Isaiah 53:5b)*

To get frankincense, cultivators slash the Sacred Boswellia trees.

This process is called "striping," and the frankincense resin bleeds out in what are called "tears" and then hardens.

The striping process alludes to the wounds Jesus suffered for us during the scourging before the crucifixion.

The first two ingredients of the Temple Incense were also related to tears, but these frankincense tears here represent us crying out not in pain, but in joy!

Frankincense represents praising God for who He is and what He has done. We all have much to praise Him for in our daily life, but by far, the greatest cause of our joy and praise is what He did for us on the cross. Because of His stripes, we have eternal life and can dwell with Him forever.

That is cause for praise even on the darkest of days, and so our prayers should always end on a note of praise.

Morning & Evening

The Temple Incense was to be burned before God on the Golden Altar every morning and every evening.

This means that we are also supposed to pray every morning and every evening. I used to think that once a day was enough. I also used to think that constantly praying throughout the day was the same thing.

It's true the Bible says to pray without ceasing, and I strongly recommend acknowledging God throughout your day. If you love Him, how can you forget about Him? If you love Him, how can you fail to acknowledge Him in all your ways?

Yet, Jesus said that when we pray, we are to go in a room by ourselves and close the door. He's clearly indicating we are to have private times of prayer, times apart from our daily life that are dedicated to praying to Him.

Christians today often call that a "quiet time." I've never been sure I liked that name for it. It's definitely a time for me to be still before Him and listen, but it's anything but a quiet time. For me, those times are the times of greatest revelation and joy.

We are to pray apart from the world every morning in order to declare that the coming day belongs to God. We are also to pray every morning as an act of worship, giving Him the firstfruits of our time.

We are to then pray again apart from the world every evening. We do this to close the day with Him, to recognize His grace and provision for us throughout the day. To seal our time as we spent it with His stamp of approval.

The God-ordained rituals described in Exodus symbolize this frequency through the daily morning and evening offerings of incense.

God is the Alpha and the Omega, the Beginning and the End. He wants our mornings *and* our evenings.

The Gold & The Wood

The Golden Altar of Incense was made of acacia (*shittim*) wood and covered with gold.

The Romans stripped branches from the acacia tree to make the Crown of Thorns.

Trees and bushes always symbolize people. The acacia symbolizes God in person (wood), the kind of wood that caused Christ pain (acacia). Jesus was crowned as our King on the cross with the crown of the painful covenant (symbolized by acacia branches) that was sealed by His blood.

Thus, acacia also always alludes to God entering into a covenant relationship with us.

The burning bush from which God spoke to Moses was an acacia. This represented the Son of God burning with the Spirit of God, initiating the Mosaic Covenant with His people.

Noah used *shittim* (acacia) wood to make the Ark, alluding to the Noahic covenant and that the person of the Messiah would provide the means of escape from God's judgment.

Three of the articles in the Tabernacle/Temple were made of acacia wood covered with gold: the Ark of the Covenant, the Table of Showbread, and the Golden Altar of Incense.

The gold covering represents the divine nature of the Kingly Christ covering His human nature (wood) with His immortal self, making Him imperishable.

Thus, through its materials, the Golden Altar of Incense shows that our prayers should be based in the person of Jesus Christ (gold covering wood). We should pray in ways that imitate Him and we should pray according to what we believe His will to be.

That is what it means to pray in Jesus' name.

The Four Horns

God mandated that the Golden Altar of Incense would be made with four horns adorning its four upper corners.

In the Bible, a horn is always a symbol for authority and the number four always symbolizes the world.

Therefore, God is symbolically saying that the prayers of God's people offered according to the will and nature of Christ have authority over this world.

This does not mean that you or I individually have authority over this world when we pray. However, it does mean that the prayers of God's people corporately do have authority over this world.

After all, Jesus said this was the case:

"Again I say to you that if two of you agree on earth concerning anything that they ask, it will be done for them by My Father in heaven. For where two or three are gathered together in My name, I am there in the midst of them." (Matthew 18:19-20)

Jesus is not telling us some magical formula here to get our way in life. He's saying that when a group of us believers are gathered *in His name*, He will be there with them. That phrase *in His name* is important. It is an old way of saying "as my representative" or "as my ambassador." Meaning, if we meet together and we meet in a sincere spirit of representing the will of Christ, He will be there in the midst of us.

And if He is there in the midst of us, His Spirit will inspire us in our prayers to pray as He would want us to. And if we are praying how He wants us to, reflecting the will of Christ Himself, then will not the Father honor our prayers and bring them to pass?

Please note that many believers come from a background where memorized prayers and repeating phrases over and over again are the standard method for praying.
This is not God's will.
In Matthew 6:7, Jesus said:

"And when you pray, do not use vain repetitions as the heathen do. For they think that they will be heard for their many words."

No, what God wants for you to do is to pray your heart. Talk to Him sincerely and tell Him whatever you're feeling. He can take it.

The bottom line is this: Pray from your heart, in private, every morning and evening. During those times, pray for God's Kingdom and the redemption of the world, for your personal needs, confess your sins to Him, and praise Him for who He is and what He has done.
And have faith that He is listening and loves you and that your prayers are effective.

Let my prayer be set before You as incense,
The lifting up of my hands as the evening sacrifice. (Psalm 141:2)

BIBLE READING PLAN

Path2Hope recommends reading at least 1-2 chapters per day in the Bible. This is the amount needed to stay fed and grow. (You can break readings up into morning & evening readings if preferred!)

Physical Bibles are preferred to digital Bibles or audio Bibles as studies have shown that we retain twice as much information when turning physical pages than with ebooks or audio books. Regardless, if those are your only option, then use them.

A believer should study the entire Bible, Old and New Testament. Below is a great Bible reading plan if you need one:

- ☐ Genesis
- ☐ Luke
- ☐ Exodus
- ☐ Acts
- ☐ Leviticus
- ☐ Hebrews
- ☐ Numbers
- ☐ Galatians
- ☐ Deuteronomy
- ☐ James
- ☐ Joshua
- ☐ Matthew
- ☐ Judges
- ☐ Romans
- ☐ Ruth
- ☐ Ephesians
- ☐ 1 & 2 Samuel
- ☐ 1 & 2 Kings
- ☐ 1 & 2 Chronicles

- ☐ Isaiah
- ☐ Jeremiah
- ☐ Lamentations
    - ☐ Psalms
    - ☐ Proverbs
    - ☐ Song of Solomon
    - ☐ Ecclesiastes
- ☐ Amos
- ☐ Joel
- ☐ Hosea
- ☐ Jonah
- ☐ Obadiah
- ☐ Micah
- ☐ Nahum
- ☐ Habakkuk
- ☐ Zephaniah
- ☐ Haggai
- ☐ Zechariah
- ☐ Malachi
- ☐ Ezekiel
- ☐ Daniel
- ☐ Ezra
- ☐ Nehemiah
- ☐ Esther
- ☐ Job
- ☐ John
- ☐ 1 & 2 Corinthians
- ☐ Philippians
- ☐ Colossians
- ☐ 1 & 2 Thessalonians
- ☐ 1 & 2 Timothy
- ☐ Philemon
- ☐ 1 & 2 Peter
- ☐ 1, 2, & 3 John

- ☐ Titus
- ☐ Jude
- ☐ Revelation

Some people like to work in the "wisdom literature" daily as well rather than read it consecutively. If you wish to do this, just add 1 chapter per day to your reading from Psalms, Proverbs, the Song of Solomon, and Ecclesiastes.

If you wish to follow a more aggressive reading plan in order to read through the entire Bible in one year, then you should daily read approximately 2 – 3 chapters in the Old Testament, 1 – 2 chapters in the New Testament, and 1 chapter from Psalms & Proverbs.

About Path2Hope

Path2Hope is dedicated to mobilizing believers to impact community for Christ.

We love seeing Christians strengthened, activated, and working to expand the Kingdom of God. We do this through four core programs:

Path2Strength – A bible-based spiritual discipleship program designed to strengthen and mobilize believers, giving them confidence to serve well.

Path2Hope Street – Neighborhood outreach teams that go door-to-door offering food & prayer, sharing the Gospel and rescuing Lost Sheep.

Redeeming Hope – Cyber teams that search for exploited women who are being sold for sex online and work to free them both physically and spiritually.

Guiding Hope – Mentors who help people suffering from significant brokenness move into healing and spiritual strength.

If you would like to help Path2Hope expand its impact for the Kingdom and see more of the work above done, please consider supporting our work at www.path2hope.org/donate

www.ingramcontent.com/pod-product-compliance
Lightning Source LLC
LaVergne TN
LVHW051520070426
835507LV00023B/3211